I Will See You Again

A Mother's Story and Sacred Journey After
Finding Her Son's Lifeless Body

Sherri Bridges Fox

BALBOA.
PRESS

A DIVISION OF HAY HOUSE

Balboa Press books may be ordered through booksellers or by contacting:

Balboa Press
A Division of Hay House
1663 Liberty Drive
Bloomington, IN 47403
www.balboapress.com
1-(877) 407-4847

Because of the dynamic nature of the Internet, any web addresses or links contained in this book may have changed since publication and may no longer be valid. The views expressed in this work are solely those of the author and do not necessarily reflect the views of the publisher, and the publisher hereby disclaims any responsibility for them.

The author of this book does not dispense medical advice or prescribe the use of any technique as a form of treatment for physical, emotional, or medical problems without the advice of a physician, either directly or indirectly. The intent of the author is only to offer information of a general nature to help you in your quest for emotional and spiritual well-being. In the event you use any of the information in this book for yourself, which is your constitutional right, the author and the publisher assume no responsibility for your actions.

Any people depicted in stock imagery provided by Thinkstock are models, and such images are being used for illustrative purposes only. Certain stock imagery © Thinkstock.

Printed in the United States of America.

ISBN: 978-1-4525-8218-4 (sc)
ISBN: 978-1-4525-8220-7 (hc)
ISBN: 978-1-4525-8219-1 (e)

Library of Congress Control Number: 2013916560

Balboa Press rev. date: 09/25/2013

Contents

Dedication

There are so many who have touched my life in profound ways. Often we are unaware of the ways in which our lives are touched, altered or changed by everyday occurrences. Sometimes it is much later that we see the blessings that have been bestowed upon us. It is with much love and appreciation that I dedicate this book.

To The Casey One, forever in my heart, forever teaching me about life and about love,

To my husband Terry, for his love, his support and his big beautiful heart, for playing his part,

To my oldest son Justin, for being the wonderful loving person and son you are, for the beautiful music that oozes from your being,

To Christy and Autumn, my special friends and neighbors who have given me their love, kindness and support,

To Rebecca, for you open mindedness and the sweetness of your open heart,

To Nikki, Avian, TJ and Grady, thank you for reminding me that family is just a heartbeat away,

To Rick for always sharing your big generous heart,

To the Dear Ones on the other side, for your loving nudges, urgings and support,

Introduction

Death is as much a part of life as living. This is my story of how death has played in and out of my life; how life itself has worked through me. It is about the death of my youngest son and how I coped. This is the story of my journey in this life, my awakening to remember that which had been hidden from me. I wish to share my story so that it may assist others on their path in this life.

I think all of us need to know that we do have a purpose in this life. It is not my intent to coerce anyone, but rather to open your mind to the many endless possibilities life offers us. Many of us search our whole lives seeking to know just what that purpose is. Although our purpose in life may seem elusive, I think it is well worth our searching to find an answer to this most important quest.

When we walk the sacred path we become aware of life on many different levels. We know and trust that the universe always conspires to assist, in ways too many to numerate. As we walk onto the path, deeper into knowing, we begin to trust our self, knowing that any questions we may have, any answers we may seek are within our grasp, awaiting acknowledgement. All life becomes sacred, knowing of the connectedness that we share in union with the One. The sacred path is not just for a select few, it is available for all; as we each awaken and begin to remember.

My sacred journey began before birth as did yours. We are each remembering our purpose in this life as we allow the light, the information to enter into our consciousness. We have only temporarily forgotten our true nature, our purpose in this life. I was not aware of my sacred journey consciously, until shortly before the death of my youngest son. It was then that I knew without a doubt, that I had to go and seek answers that would assist me with my life, what I did not consciously know is that I was being assisted with, and prepared for, the physical departure of my son. It is this sacred journey that has propelled me into another way of being, another way of knowing and living. It is this knowledge that has allowed me to find peace and happiness after the loss I felt when finding his lifeless body in his room that morning. It is a journey that I will be on for the rest of my physical life on this earth. I can only hope that the details of my spiritual journey can assist others to find their spiritual path in this life, to know there is light at the end of the tunnel.

The time is upon us now and the energies are present within our earthly plane, our bodies and the body of mother earth. The energies of December 21, 2012 signaled a great time in the history of the universe as all the planets and the stars aligned to bring us into the Age of Aquarius. Over the next twenty to twenty-five years we who are present here on earth are destined for great changes, changes within ourselves. We are preparing and paving the path for these changes. Many of us have remembered and many more will remember. There is so much more to us humans, this earth and our history. It has been kept from us. Many documents of our history have been destroyed. It is the word of mouth from our indigenous people that have kept the truth alive, passing it down from generation to generation.

We have been controlled by the powers that be and we have been lead to believe that we are weak and powerless. We are only using ten percent of our brains. Why do you think that is? We have DNA that scientist call junk DNA. Why would we only use a portion of our DNA? We have visitors from the skies that many have seen and yet it is kept from us. Surely we do not really believe that there is not more to our universe than our small little world. We have been living in a fear so controlling that most of us do not even know that we are being controlled. We do not realize that our minds are shut. Why do you think that is? I don't believe our creator makes mistakes. We were created in love and have the God gene within our bodies. We are co-creators with God. What will happen when we come to the realization that: We are all family?

It is up to each and every one of us to find our truth, our path in this life. It is up to us to be forever mindful, to be aware of our emotions, our thoughts and how they affect everything in creation. We are the ones that have come into this life to make the changes on planet earth that will forever change life as we have come to know it.

Our planet and our lives are both wonderful and magical. Miracles happen every day! Do not be afraid to step forward into spirit and let the old ways be forever gone as we embrace ourselves and our divine heritage from Mother/Father God.

Our unique gift of emotion, of remembering and connecting with the other dimensions has been passed down in the analogs of time. We are preparing an Earth life that will anchor many eons of love, acceptance and remembrance to welcome our star nations into our earthly lives with love and respect. We will no longer have wars, especially wars over our religious beliefs. We will and we can, accept our differences and love one another as we are. We can do it. You can do it.

Transformation

I refer to the internal change that I underwent over the past four years as a transformation. We all have an idea of what transformation means; a change or process of changing from one way of being into another. Transformation implies that the end result will be a positive one. Just as the butterfly begins life as an egg, then a chrysalis and emerges into this breathtakingly beautiful creature, its' final stage having no resemblance with the creature it began life as.

During the time that the butterfly is a chrysalis it appears from the outside that nothing is going on, but there is great change taking place from within. It took me a while to realize that I too, had great changes that were taking place within. It was only when I could look back and see old beliefs and patterns that were no longer a part of my world that I realized my change from within. As it was happening I was completely unaware that my transformation was under way.

I was well into learning about spirit, about myself before I would even know that I had changed from one way of being into another. At no time was I afraid or overwhelmed in any kind of way while going deeper and deeper into my understanding of spirit, of myself. When I speak of Spirit, the Universe or the unseen world,

I am referring to our creator, Mother/Father God, The All That Is, the Divine or those on the other side. There are many names which refer to the same thing and I do not think that it matters the name that we choose to call our Beloved. I believe that our creator has many helpers in the unseen world who are given the task of assisting those who may have asked, those that are ready to awaken as part of their journey in this life. My journey and any journey of awakening to spirit is always filled with love and respect; love of the being that we are at the present moment and for the being we are becoming.

Spirit is truth to me, in the deepest sense of the word. When discovering one's truth and working with spirit; there is never any judgment, condemnation, shame, or guilt that is used to manipulate one in any way whatsoever. Spirit is our creator's way of taking us by the hand and leading us gently and lovingly. Our divine awareness is always of the heart. When I work with spirit, I am working with God, the Divine white light from which we came.

I am writing to you about what was a very difficult time in my life and the events that changed my views of self, of life as I knew it and death as I perceived it. I am writing about experiences that are very personal and dear to my heart, the death of my youngest child, the events leading up to his death and the events that happened after his death. I am describing my feelings with you as I remember them at the time of his passing. I am sharing with you, my feelings of deep hurt and profound loss that I felt when I found my son's body. Not only was I having all of these feelings over perceiving his death as a tragic loss, I was also experiencing the shock of finding my son's dead body. You will read about the chain of events that changed my life and the life of my family forever. This was the most difficult period in my life, but as I would learn, it also turned into one of the most wonderful and life altering experiences of my life as I allowed Spirit to lead me onto my sacred journey. Many of us will find ourselves in these very circumstances, with the worst of times and the best of times both happening congruently. It is up to us how we are going to juggle the two extremes and find balance in our life. What may seem like one of the darkest of times may lead you into one of the brightest times of your life.

I could never have imagined the depth of feelings and emotions I experienced, having one of my children to pass from this earth before me. I just knew how much I loved my two sons and wanted to protect them from any perceived danger. It was scary for me just to think that something could happen to hurt them, to take them from me, their death was not anything that I ever allowed myself to imagine. For parents and grandparents, any of us who have children in our lives, they feel like they are our world. We love, hold, and cling to them for fear of losing them; for seemingly they are the most precious beings that we have. I call them our most precious commodity on earth, our shining jewels, but what we forget is that, we adults, were and are those same precious jewels in a grown up body. We forget our own inner beauty and worth. We forget that inner child still lives within our body waiting to be recognized.

To imagine losing one of my sons, was just something so horrific, that I could not even phantom such a loss. To lose a child can be one of life's most difficult challenges to recover from. To lose any of our loved ones can be very traumatic for us. We have been brought up to see death as the end of a life, something awful and sad. I want you to know that it does not have to feel this way. We are all going to have death to be a part of our lives. There is no need to fear death, for now, it is how we take our exit from this earth, we return from where we came.

As parents, most of us have expectations of seeing our children grown, becoming adults, settling down, getting married and maybe having children of their own. As parents, we may often expect to pass from this earth before our children. All of these hopes and dreams seem to make the loss of a child even more difficult, as the pain can be indescribable, and at times unbearable. I am writing about the events that took place in my life and the perspective I had at the time of my son's passing, how these perspectives have changed and how I have changed.

I am forever grateful for the Divine Intervention of Spirit and the unseen world. I am also grateful for all of the loving family and friends that were put onto my path in perfect timing, bringing messages from beyond, messages I would learn to allow, interpret and appreciate. I have learned to incorporate these beautiful gifts of the universe into my life, allowing them to prepare, guide and assist me along my path.

I hope that in writing to you about losing my child that I will be able to assist those of you who have lost someone to death move through your grief. I wish to help you find ways to express your grief in your own personal way and to assure you that we all grieve in our own way, in our own time. Even more than moving beyond the grief of death I want to assist you in seeing death from a different and broader perspective.

Although the death of my youngest son was the situation I found myself drowning in, there are many life situations that can happen that may leave us feeling injured, hurt, victimized, overwhelmed, guilty, depressed or angry. This is just a few of the negative emotions that we may have that can send us into a downward spiral from which it may seem or feel impossible to return from.

I will be presenting you with some of the tools and habits that will allow you to move past all of the negative events, memories and emotions that you think may have you trapped. If you are ready, we will be working with some exercises later on that will assist you to move on with your life in a positive way. Please know that we are all capable of finding peace, happiness and joy in our lives, although it may feel like an elusive desire for some of you at this time in your life. I will ask you to keep an open mind and read the book through to the end and be prepared to do a little work on yourself. You are so worth it. You can do it. I am here for you. I understand and feel your pain.

We are going to learn how to work through, allow, and let go of the thoughts, feelings and emotions that bring us down. When we deny the emotions that we feel, we are in effect denying a part of ourselves to be expressed, this is what sets us up for illness and eventually, disease. It is in experiencing our emotions as they occur, even as painful as they may feel at the time, that we are allowing ourselves to be who we are, to experience and feel, thus allowing ourselves to heal. Feel the emotions and let them go. Let them go! They will be replaced by other emotions.

As I share my journey of spirit with you throughout the many stages of my life, I hope you will see how spirit ever gently plays in and out of our lives. I am also going to introduce you to a most beautiful and wonderful place, I call Serenity Farm Retreat, my childhood home. I am going to present you with the passing of my mother, my youngest son and while I was sharing my journey with you, most recently, the passing of my father. I was at very different places about my perspectives of life, death and dying when each of my loved ones passed. It was my thoughts and how I perceived death with each passing that played such a huge role in my understanding and allowance of their death and the perception of grief I experienced.

At the time of Casey's passing I had just begun going deeper into my spiritual journey, into deeper knowing and understanding of the unseen world. Again, I am forever grateful for the divine intervention that assisted me to eventually see, allow and accept my son's passing with an understanding that is eternal. I feel that if I had not been at such a place in my enfoldment that I would have slit my wrists from the grief and agony that I would have felt and clung to, without the intervention of higher guidance.

After Casey's death, I was aware that I was never alone; the unseen world of spirit was always with me when I needed them. Almost every time I shut my eyes I saw a beautiful magenta color and was aware that I was being held in love. I was not alone. Although I did not understand all that was happening with me at the time, I knew that it was something most wonderful. I am sharing my story in hopes that it may inspire, heal and motivate those that it touches. Loving assistance is always present from the other side, in the unseen world of spirit. I like to call them God's assistants.

I am telling you my personal story and presenting you with some of the tools that will assist you in gaining control of your life through being empowered. Sit back, relax, and get ready to peel back the layers of entrapment. We are much like the onion which has many layers, each one revealing another part of its self. We are going to go deeper and deeper into our center, the spiritual heart where we will find our truest self. When we allow ourselves to just be and stop the judgment, the expectations of the people in our lives, of life, we are free to just be and experience life as it comes. We can use our "paddles", our knowing, to navigate our life, instead of being adrift in the sea of life. We can begin to appreciate all the small and beautiful moments life offers us.

It is important that you know within your whole being that you can be happy, and that YOU deserve peace, happiness and joy in your life. Joy is our natural state as beings of light. I want you to know that you are so much more than you think you are. You are capable, loveable and powerful, yes powerful! The ball will be in your court, it is your life and your decision on how you choose to use these tools. Life goes on. Our choices in life always effect our lives and also have a ripple effect to all of those around us and to the vibration of the whole universe. Everything is alive and part of the ALL THAT IS.

I am a counselor by choice, but I cannot help someone who does not want to help themselves, nor can you. We can only extend our hand, while offering our compassion and understanding. We can only listen with an open heart and forego our judgment. We can recognize that all of us are on a chosen path and honor that path while trying to see the big picture, not the finite picture our personality self may want us to see. Acceptance of one another is something we all want. Come take my hand and let us walk together.

My Mother, Anne

I, just as you, carry the memories of my mother in my heart and my mind, but I just as you, also carry her memories in my blood, my very cells, my DNA, not only do I carry my mother's memories, but I also carry the memories of my families heritage. We all carry our heritage within our bodily vessel. It is not just our physical family heritage we carry, but also our soul's other aspects from the many, many sojourns in and out of life. We have been going in and out of life from our very existence. The soul is eternal. We see ourselves as only this personality, as separate, but there is so much more to each and every one of us. There are many ways of living, of being.

I wish to tell you the story of my mother, her passing and how I perceived her death. I had not yet gone into the depth of my journey of spirit on which I found myself with the passing of my youngest son. I perceived her death quite differently. I want to share with you how my thoughts, our thoughts, create our reactions in life.

A little over thirteen years ago, in January of 2000, I lost my mother to Alzheimer's disease. She had been a victim to this disease for several years. She passed at the age of eighty five and up until a few years before Alzheimer's and dementia came on, she lived a very active life.

When my mother was seven years old her father was in a serious accident at the tanning factory where he worked. He was brought home to die. A doctor was summoned and he came to the house. Her father passed within three days, leaving her mother and the other seven children in extreme poverty. Life was already a difficult existence, with the father working. Food was scarce and the quality of life was difficult, at best. His death was a hard financial blow for the entire family. It was 1922, the whole country was in a state of rapid decline and poverty was a way of life for many. To help ease the hardship and financial burden on my grandmother, my mother was sent to live with her older sister Clementine, nine years her senior. Clementine was already out of the house and married. Whatever her sister, Clemmy told her to do, she did; clean, cook, milk the cow, rake the yard, wash clothes. All of the younger kids were afraid of Clementine. She inflicted fear into their minds; therefore this fear was also a part of their lives. She was like a mean, arrogant dictator to the kids. Clementine always told my mother how ugly she was, that her hair was piss burnt brown. She was always belittling her in any way that she could while bossing her around. It wasn't just my mother she teased and tormented, she belittled all of her younger siblings. She was obviously a very angry person and took it out on her brothers and sisters. She had no children of her own.

We went to visit my Aunt Clemmy on many occasions when I was a child. She happened to live beside my grandmother. She was a force to be reckoned with. I found myself being very afraid of her. My most embedded memory of her was when I was around seven years old. We had gone to her house for a family gathering. That day she took me with her to the rabbit hutches. I was excited to see all of her rabbits. There was cage after cage. She told me how to tell the difference between a boy rabbit and a girl rabbit. She explained that the boys have what looks like the end of a sharp pencil between their legs. She picked up one of the younger rabbits, as she held the small little furry creature in her arms she showed me he was a male. Before I knew it, she had twisted his little neck, ending his life before my eyes. She said he was our main course for dinner that day. I had a lump in my throat that kept me from swallowing right after that. I thought she loved the little critters like I did. It turned out that she and I had different concepts about the rabbits.

Just like her older sister, at the age of fourteen my mother became a married woman. She delivered her first child by the age of fifteen. Mama told me this baby had brought her so much joy, a joy I sensed she needed in her life. She said he was a happy baby and was always smiling. I would not know the whole story of her marriage until I was grown. Mother told me on her wedding day, very much to her surprise, her new mother-in-law said she was glad that her son was getting married and would be hitting someone else. Mama said soon after they were married he started hitting her! She said he would get very angry and just blow up, and take it out on her. She began working in a factory soon after she was married. As I grew up and put the pieces together I knew that he was an alcoholic and that he had beaten her and had run around on her with other women. She was pregnant with the fourth baby when he had beaten her so badly that she lost this baby. He was a boy. It was ten years later that my brother Jerry was born.

As I reflect back on her life I know that she must have felt so alone and alienated with nowhere to turn to escape, or no one to turn to for help. I am sure my grandmother was there for her emotionally, listening and understanding, but unable to help her in any physical or financial way. She was barely getting by feeding and taking care of the other kids. My mother was no more than a child herself when she married, although I am sure she never really felt like a child. I am not so sure she ever just got to play, have fun and be a child. She always felt responsible for helping with the care of the younger children in her family, easing the burden for her mother.

As a child I had always noticed a scar on my Mother's belly. It was a rather large scar, about ten inches long on the right side of her lower abdomen. I asked her many times if it was from me being born. She usually ignored my question until one day she muttered a yes. I think she was just trying to get me to quit asking because I just wouldn't let it go. I later learned that it was from a surgery, one that had saved her life. It seems she finally did leave her first husband, getting a place of her own. She had begun to date other men. One evening the door bell rang, she answered the door, and it was him, her first husband. He stepped inside the door not saying a word and as he did, he stabbed her several times in the stomach with a pocket knife and just ran away. She collapsed to the floor. She was rushed to the hospital and underwent surgery to repair the damage. My brother, who was around five years of age at the time, vaguely remembers it. He remembers being scared and being alone for a period of time. She almost died from the stab wounds. As I matured she eventually started to talk to me and tell me things about her marriage to him. She told me about how she hid money for the first baby so she could pay the mid wife. She said he found it and spent it on alcohol. At one time she said they had moved to Maryland for work. She said she used to take the kids to see their father play ball. She said he was a good ball player, but couldn't stop drinking long enough to be serious about the game. My brother Jerry was born in Maryland. The family soon returned to Statesville. Mama told me about one of the most hurtful memories she had was when my sister Carol Sue was about to be married. She said she was walking in down town Statesville and overheard two women talking about my sister, Carol Sue. What they said broke my mother's heart. Mama said she felt ashamed. She overheard them saying something like this, "You know Carol Sues' mother is that old Annie S., she was married to that drunk, Glen. He was always running around on her." Mama said she felt so small, so embarrassed. My heart ached for her. She had no control over him, yet she was judged by his actions, not hers.

She remained married to her first husband for almost twenty years before leaving on her own. When I was young I just couldn't believe she had stayed with him so long after the way he had treated her from the very beginning of their life together. I just didn't have any life experience with which to relate. I am sure she did the best she could at the time. I asked her why she didn't leave him sooner. As a young adult, I didn't realize she had her children to think about, feed and take care of. It was, in the taking care of her four children and putting their needs before her own, that got her through those hard and difficult years, taking her mind away from her own misery and hardship.

As a child, I thought Mama's first husband was a monster. I mean a real monster, scary looking and ugly, in my child's mind. When I was nine years old my sister Jan was watching me for the day, she had to take me with her when she went to the hospital to see her father, he was on his death bed. I really wondered why she even wanted to see such a monster. As a child, I was forgetting that he was her father. I remember as I looked at him in the hospital bed, I thought; he's just a man, a little old man. To her that was her father, a man she loved.

Mama had a hard and difficult childhood and adult life. She had told me about the things that had happened in her life, as a matter of fact. I do not remember any anger, resentment or sadness in her voice. Much of it I had learned just by listening to my mother, sisters and brothers conversations, putting pieces together on my own over the course of years. I knew my mother had a strong will and whatever she would set her mind to do she would get it done. I knew this as a child. As I look back and reflect on her demeanor about all of those horrible things that were done to her, her childhood, her mean sister and the husband who had treated her so badly, she was not bitter. She had moved on. She had moved away from it and it did not define who she was. She made herself a new life. She had not forgotten any of it, but she had let it go. These memories did not control her life. They were just memories filed away. It was not until writing down these words about her that I realized she had moved own with her life. She had set the example for me to do the same with my own life. Rather than dwell on negative past events, move own and live your life. She had not forgotten any of those bad times; she could talk about them with ease and grace. There was no bitterness in her voice. It was just the way it was.

Mama dated and remained single almost ten years. At the age of forty she married a second time to a man who was seven years her junior, my father. They met in Statesville, at a local dance for the service men. She caught my father's eye that night and even though he couldn't dance all that well, they struck up a conversation and as the story goes, the rest is history. They could not have dated very long. I found it very hard to believe that my father, who had never been married, would marry a lady seven years his senior with grown children.

Unlike the description her sister had given my mother, I had been told by many that my mother was an extremely attractive woman. She had fair skin with dark auburn hair, her eyes the color of the ocean. She stood about five foot, one and a half inches tall. She had an hour glass figure from what I had been told. At the age of 33, it was my father's first marriage. He was on leave from the service for a short duration, so needless to say, it was a very short engagement. They were married right away before he was to be shipped off to Okinawa, Japan. I was conceived in love and born while he was at sea.

Growing up I was always aware of her age and the fact that she was much older than the mothers of my friends. I was always explaining to the kids at school how I was an Aunt with nieces and nephews. Although she did not look older than the other mothers, I knew her age and how much older she was than my father. In my little child's mind I created this fear of her dying while I was a child and leaving me alone, without her. I told no one. I kept those scary thoughts to myself. They brought me much sadness and fear to even think about her not being here with me. As a child I allowed my fears and worries about her dying to upset me. It was something I had created in my mind. I would often cry myself to sleep with those thoughts on my mind. I didn't want to tell anyone because in my mind it would only make it more real. As I grew older I eventually let go of those self imposed, childish thoughts. I realized that they were thoughts I had created.

She had been my mother, my friend and my companion for so long, but as I saw what the Alzheimer's was taking from her, doing to her, I began to let go of my grip of wanting to hang on to her and prepared myself to let her go. We had moved from the farm several years earlier when Terry, my husband, had taken a job in the Raleigh area. He had in lived in an apartment, driving 150 miles, back and forth to Statesville on the weekends. One day while looking at photos with baby Casey, we came to a picture of his Daddy, I had asked, "Who is this?" his reply, "Daddy gone." I told Mama about it and she said we needed to be together as a family. It was so hard to leave my mother and father and the farm. We moved from Statesville soon after. Both of our sons were young, Justin was seven and Casey was less than two, before that we had lived on the farm, within walking distance from my house to my family home. It was very difficult for me to move from my family. I was comfortable and it was the only life I had known. I would cry every time we would leave for home after visiting with mama and daddy. Mama would come to visit us often after our move and would stay for several weeks at a time. Through the years as the Alzheimer's progressed she was no longer able to leave her familiar environment of home. She had told my Father that she may as well go ahead and die because she could not beat this problem.

We usually came home to visit every two weeks of so, or as often as possible. As the Alzheimer's progressed and stole more and more of her memory, I would come and sit beside her on the sofa. When she had tears in her eyes I knew she was thinking about leaving us behind. She seemed so scared and sad. I wanted to reassure her. I told her she would not be alone. I told that her family and the angels would be there, on the other side to greet her. She knew this already, I was just reminding her. I could tell she liked hearing and being reminded that her family would be there as she was the last sibling to pass. Her frown released and she began to smile.

On our last family visit, before her passing, she was like her old self when we arrived. She was smiling. She was clear headed and sharp, hugging all of us and asking how we had been, calling us by name. It was a marker, a turning point; I called my brother Jerry so that he could make the drive from Wilmington and say his last farewells before she was gone. Her clarity was short lived, only lasting for a few hours and then the dementia of Alzheimer's was with her again.

Almost two weeks after our return home she had called me. It was unusual because she had not been able to call me for a long while. I usually called and talked to her. It would be our last phone conversation together. As we talked it was obvious that she had clarity of mind again. The conversation was very short and then she said; "I love you. I love you. I love you." It overwhelmed me, as I could feel those words I had not gotten to hear for so long, go straight to my heart. I felt a big lump in my throat and tears welling up in my eyes. I said; "We love you." I knew I would lose myself with a tidal wave of emotion and tears if I had said, "I" love you. I did not want to upset her by sobbing. Again, I felt that her time was nearing and that her clarity was yet another gift, another chance for closure with this life.

I began calling her each day after our last call. I was so sure that something was about to happen. My father would answer the phone and he had told me on two occasions that she could not come to the phone. He was very vague. I did not get to talk with her again after our last phone conversation. I was upset that I wasn't there myself. I called in reinforcements. I had my sister, Jan and my niece, Dawn to go out to the house and report back to me. She had taken a serious decline, only taking in small amounts of food and water. She was not, or could not talk.

I tried to prepare myself for her passing. I wanted to be by her side when it was her time to pass. Within days Hospice was called in to take care of her. Terry and I along with the boys were home bound to see her before she passed. We just wanted to be there with her and daddy. We found ourselves returning home in one of the worst snow storms to hit North Carolina in many years. Our normal drive of two and a half hours took six hours. Terry had to pull our vehicle into the shelter of a car wash and put RainX on the windshield so that we could have some visibility. He knew the importance and value of me being with her, as he also wanted to be by her side. When we arrived she could not be roused. I said a few words to her without any response. I felt like I was bothering her, intruding on her private time with the other side. She was working and preparing to go to the unseen world. I understood. She did not have to say a word to me. I just wanted to be near her. Terry had taken her by the hand and told her that we would take care of Bob, my father. He told her not to worry about him. We gathered around her and gave her our love. It was very soon thereafter that we saw her take her last breath. There was no resistance, and then she was gone. Hospice was there for four days. Her death certificate read cause of death; "Ceased to Thrive."

The Alzheimer's, her quality of life, her age and her willingness to go to the unseen world, all made her passing a little easier for me to accept. She was eighty five years old at the time of her passing. All of these thoughts allowed me to let her go to the other side more easily. It did not mean that I did not grieve her passing. I cried and whaled for days as all of it seemed surreal. When I read her obituary in the paper, I felt like someone had hit me between the eyes. I didn't want to believe what I was reading. I didn't want it to be real at all. I would need my time to grieve for her, to let her go. After her passing, I stayed with my father for the next week to help him get settled a bit. He told me, "It would take some getting used to." That was his way of telling me he would miss her, not having her by his side. Terry had taken the boys back home to Raleigh and would return for me later, giving me a chance to be alone with daddy.

Although I did prepare myself mentally to let her go, I was letting her go for logical reasons that made sense to me. Logically, I knew the Alzheimer's would only get worse. She was ready to accept death and I knew she was getting up in years. I was not remembering her as the soul. I was seeing her as my mother and knew she had a soul. I was not prepared to look at her death from the perspective of the soul; I only looked at her passing from the logical perspective. It was my perspective at the time, although my thought pattern did assist me in letting her go, in accepting her death.

Let me tell you a little bit more about my mother. She was a beautiful inspiration for many. In her later years she baby sat for many of the young mothers in Statesville. She would baby sit and clean the house as if it were her own. It was her way of going the extra mile and helping those young mothers out. She was never one to just sit on her bum. Word of her work and babysitting skills flew through Statesville. She was in demand and was always busy babysitting for someone. She also kept the younger ones for the preschool. She dearly loved those little children and they would call her "B", much easier to say than Mrs. Bridges, her last name. She once told me the story of a five year old boy she was babysitting for the first time. She said he kept staring at her and looking at her. She asked him; "You have not been close to an old person, have you?" He replied, "no". She told him it was okay if he wanted to touch the skin on her face or her hands. She understood just how strange her wrinkles looked to this little guy who had not been near an older person. She was so very good with the little ones.

My Mother was also an exceptional cook, making her dishes from scratch and always using natural ingredients. She loved to prepare a huge meal for the whole family on Sundays and special occasions. It was one of her favorite ways to give you her love. There was always more food than our extended family could eat at one sitting. Our family "get togethers" was an event that the whole family looked forward to. She would make the best tasting cakes, but they usually looked like "leaning towers of pizza". Sometimes you had to be really careful not to eat a toothpick that was holding the cake together. We would all make jokes and laugh at some of her cakes, but no matter what, they always, without a doubt, tasted good. She fried the most mouth watering southern fried chicken. I can still taste it. Her fried chicken would disappear at the family reunions and Sunday lunch. She would usually hide the fried chicken from my father on Sundays, who remained at home while we went to church. She made her biscuits from scratch; they just melted in your mouth. She really never used recipes, but would make her dishes as she went, from memory. We videotaped her making biscuits so we could learn and remember. She always told me that the dough needed to feel like a "baby's butt" to the touch, or you had worked your dough too much and the biscuits would be tough. She would place self rising four, Crisco shortening and milk into a bowl, mixing it all together by hand and by feel and experience. She and Terry spent a lot of time in the kitchen preparing meals together throughout the years before her passing.

I cannot leave out the beautiful gardens that my Mother had and tended to. Mama's gardens were always a place of spectacular beauty here on the farm. It was her gardening that brought beauty and color to the farm where there had been none. She put many hard and loving hours into her gardens, watering most with a five gallon bucket and pulling weeds by hand and hoe. She could root almost any flower or cutting that could be rooted. If she saw something in someone's yard that caught her eye, she would not hesitate to stop and ask if they would mind sharing it with her as she was always willing to share her plants with others. She thought everyone would do the same with her. I remember as a child I would get so embarrassed when she would stop the car and ask a complete stranger who happened to be in their garden, to share a flower or a plant that had caught her eye. She had a natural talent for arranging flowers. She had a reputation for her beautiful fresh cut flower bouquets. If there was a flower in bloom, we had a vase of flowers in the house. It was so wonderful to have fresh flowers in the house. I loved to see her bouquets and smell the fragrance of the flowers. She would always take flowers in bloom in a beautiful vase to the church on Sunday mornings. I have my Mother to thank for my interest in and knowledge of gardening.

I think my Mother had gone through some very rough times in her younger years. I used to tell my sisters that I had a different mother than the one they knew. Life was different for her and she was different. She was older and carrying the wisdom of experience. I knew I was the lucky one. I want to thank her for her beautiful attitude towards life and her strong will. I like to think I got my attitude and will from her example. She is never far from my heart.

The Move to Wilmington

Our move to Wilmington was like a new beginning, a starting over place after mama's passing. It was like a big mystery waiting to happen and unfold before our eyes. We were excited. Mama had always traveled with us when she was well and now we had to go on without her. We were looking forward to being closer to my brother and sister-n-law, my two nephews and their wives. Terry and the boys were so excited to be near the beach. We had planned this move to the coast in an effort to assist Justin pursue a musical career. He started playing the guitar when he was thirteen and he had learned very quickly. He was quite good. His cousin Jeremy, who was the drummer, already lived in Wilmington. There were also two gentlemen in Wilmington that were retired from the music scene that had heard Justin and the guys. They wanted to help promote them.

We arrived in Wilmington in the spring of 2001. Terry and Justin rented a tiny little apartment close to downtown Wilmington. Casey and I went to live at the farm with daddy until we couldn't stand being apart from the Terry and Justin. Casey and I packed our belongings and headed to Wilmington too. We moved into the tiny little apartment with Terry and Justin. It wasn't long until we were busting out of it and felt we could no longer live in the tight quarters.

The four of us were in the apartment for only a few weeks when we decided that we might as well buy a house. We found an older home that was built in 1914. The house had a lot of character and historic touches. It also had a detached mother-in-law suite. The mother-in-law suite was very; very small, but would suit our needs perfectly. It had one bedroom and one bath, with a very, very small living room and the smallest kitchen I have ever seen. It would only be Justin living there and it was right out the back door of the house, making me feel a lot easier, having him close by. The whole yard was fenced in and it backed up to an old drive that had been used as the garbage collection alley. It would be the perfect place to practice music.

On the day of the move into the new house Casey turned 10 years old. Terry was in the hospital. He had fallen from the roof of the new house while coming down the ladder after doing repairs on the roof. I had pulled into the driveway just in time to see it all transpire. I felt like I was watching a movie. Time stood still as I watched, unable to do anything. I got out of the car and walked closer just in time to see Terry lifting the lower part of his leg off of a tree limb. I screamed and looked up to see a neighbor coming around the house. She had an ice pack in her hand, ready for us to immediately place it onto Terry's leg. We were off and headed to the emergency room. Friends and family came the next day. They helped me and the boys get moved into the house while Terry lay in a hospital bed. It was a not so happy birthday for Casey. Needless to say, there was a lot going on that day.

We were in a transitional, older neighborhood and we were the minority. Casey was very happy there and made many friends quickly. Whenever we would be out and about together in the neighborhood or at the community store we would most often hear; "What up Case?" He was accepted in the hood, honored and protected by the local guys. There just happened to be a big park nearby and that is where Casey spent a lot of time and got to know the local neighborhood guys. He was always out of doors as much as we would allow him to be gone.

While we were in the apartment we had set up a vivarium for the green anoles. Anoles are little lizards that are indigenous to the southeastern United States. They can change their color from green to brown depending on the background. The male anoles have a bright red flab of skin under the throat that is called a dewlap. They do a kind of push up movement and "blow" up the dewlap to attract the female. This vivarium was for Casey. He was always interested in nature. These beautiful little green lizards were everywhere in Wilmington. They did not seem to mind being held with gentle hands. Casey was the nature boy and he seemed to be holding some animal or creature all the time. We had three anoles, two females and one male. We had read that it was very difficult to breed anoles in captivity. We explained this to Casey and told him that we may not have baby anoles. Casey understood and we all agreed we would set them free after we moved into the new house. We had not been in the house very long when the day came that we set the anoles loose in the backyard. The empty vivarium had been setting in Casey's bedroom for several weeks. As I was cleaning his bedroom one day, Sissy our big gray girl cat had jumped on top of it and had begun switching her tail back and forth. I told her it was empty, but she would not listen, she knew better and kept on looking at it intently. So, I thought I needed to see what had her attention. As I looked closer I saw several teeny, tiny, little baby anoles! They had hatched without our even knowing they were there. We would peel bananas and let them set out to attract gnats to feed our little babies. We were all so very proud of our little baby anoles. They were our little miracles. Again, we agreed to set the baby anoles free after they were a little bigger and could find food for themselves.

As we continued to settle in the guys were busy playing different gigs around town and out of town. Although Terry was still recovering from his accident, he still continued to play in the band as the bass player and back up vocalist. Many gigs were played with him on crutches. Justin was the lead guitar player and singer for the band. At the time he was sixteen. He dressed in the most colorful and loud clothes, usually wearing a red hat and wingtip shoes. His cousin Jeremy was the drummer and back up vocalist as well. Justin was quite the sensation in the Wilmington area. His bigger than life talent, stage presence and his young age always seemed to draw a big crowd. People were always interested in the fact that Justin's father was part of the band and his little brother Casey was there at the gig, playing pool usually. I was always there supporting the guys and keeping an eye on Casey. At the time "Justin Fox and Catfish Lane" played the blues, doing a lot of Stevie Ray Vaughn cover songs. Watching Justin play the blues is like watching the music flow to him straight from the heavens. We traveled about the town and surrounding communities and the state for several years.

Casey and I always tagged along when we could, although playing music was quite challenging financially. A gig in the Virgin Islands was offered with accommodations provided. We thought it would be a great family vacation; we bought tickets so that Casey and I got to go on this very special trip. It was Casey's first plane ride. We boarded at the Wilmington airport and then were re-routed to Charlotte Douglas International Airport. I remember it was a stormy day. The plane was experiencing a lot of turbulence. Many people were holding to their seats with white knuckles showing as we landed in Charlotte. I looked over at Casey and he was grinning, his dimples showing. He was having fun. Most everyone on the plane was scared and nervous and he thought it was fun. I guess if you thought of our unusually bumpy trip as a Disney ride it would have been fun. After the initial bumpy ride we were headed straight for the Virgin Islands. It was a little lengthy, but it was a smooth ride. We landed without incident. It was a beautiful tropical island. We could see the blue green waters from the air changing colors as the water got shallower. As soon as we landed we began instantly taking in the scenery. I found the buildings to be of little interest, but the vegetation, that is another story. We rented a car and packed into it like sardines, one after the other. It was a little bit of a challenge to drive on the opposite side of the road than we normally do here in the States, but round and round and round the mountain we went up to the house where we would stay for the week. There were many houses nestled into the side of the mountain, but one had to really look to see any of the houses through the lush tropical vegetation. We were met at the house by the caretaker. He educated us on the use of the cistern. To conserve water, we were not to flush the toilet for a single number one use, only number two's were to be flushed immediately. These instructions felt foreign and kind of yucky to us as the time, but one has to understand to conserve water, changes must be made. The cistern has been in use for thousands of years. Some of us are spoiled in the United States, taking our water for granted.

We hurried to get settled into our guest quarters that afternoon and be ready for the guys to perform in the evening at a local pub. It was a very hot and sultry summer night. Casey wanted to get into the small pool that was there and take a swim, but the water was so cold that even he could not take it. The guys were playing gigs every night that we were there on the island. There were many, many late hours. During the day we would go to the local beach hangout and play in the ocean and the guys would snorkel. The smell of marijuana was prevalent everywhere. Justin would receive many "pot" gifts for his playing.

For one of the gigs, we had to travel to another smaller island, the British side of the Virgin Islands. We spent two days on this island. Most all the structures had architectural details and were very colorful and beautiful. This smaller island was very quaint and had a more relaxed feel. After the gig was over we had to travel back to the main island; it was very, very late at night. It seems there had been no rooms available for us to stay over another night; our reservations were a little mixed up. The only transportation choice we had available to us, (if we didn't want to sleep in the sand on the beach), was to travel in a small boat that did not have any lights! We carried our overnight luggage, removed our shoes and walked down into the water, up to our knees and boarded onto the boat. We crowded into this small boat, along with Justin's guitars, sitting along the edge and wherever we could find something to hold onto. There was no seating. No, we did not have any life vests on! No, I am not a good swimmer. I was prepared to bend over and kiss life goodbye. I put the situation into the powers that be. We took off and remained at a fairly high rate of speed; we didn't just putt along. All I could see was darkness everywhere I tried to find light, until finally we came closer to the main island and I could see some faint lights in the distance. I pried my hands off the edge of the boat where I was hunched down to take my leave. My knees were shaking, as I exited from the boat. I was scared, to say the least, and I would not like to experience this again. It seems I do not like being on a body of water not knowing where I am going or being able to see where I am going. I just had to relinquish my control and trust the guy steering the boat. He had probably made the trip so many times that "he could do it in the dark".

Overall the trip was wonderful! We ate lots and lots of good food and local fresh fruit. We got to have lots of water activities. We saw beautiful and exotic fish. We were invited as guests on a huge yacht for dinner. We got to see the huge island iguanas up front and personal, as one walked in between Justin and his suitcase without him seeing it. The poor iguana was given a big spin around. We also saw the poverty of the the locals and it hurt us to see it, but we also knew tourism brought an exchange of money to this island.

After we got back home to Wilmington we unpacked and were settling in. We were about to have a most unexpected surprise. I was unpacking my camera, as I brought out the camera case there before my eyes, was a very small little baby gecko that had hitched a ride from the Virgin Islands. It was stuck to some tape I had used to secure a piece of camera equipment. I called for Terry and the boys. I was giddy and so were they. I could not believe this little baby gecko had survived a plane trip from the Virgin Islands to North Carolina, in a camera case, stuck to a piece of tape. It was so very tiny and stuck firmly to the tape. I guess being secured to the tape was like wearing a seat belt. Terry had to work so very carefully to loosen this little baby without hurting him or doing any major damage. The gecko did lose a little bit of his spots, but he seemed OK, very alert and ready to go, we set him free outside the house. We left this one to the powers that be.

As we settled back into our little routines we were beginning to feel a bit tight, financially. Terry had gladly given up his job as a sales consultant before for our move to Wilmington, a job that had gone corporate. He had no regrets about leaving his job of ten years. We lived off of our savings for as long as we could. When the money started to get low we decided to buy a fixer upper house and turn it over and sell it for a profit. This idea was a little scary for us, we hadn't bought a house with the intention of selling it/ flipping it for a profit, but we had faith that we could pull it off and we did. We were always doing and fixing things ourselves. We invested quite a bit of sweat equity, but we did it. We sold our first investment house for a profit that would keep us comfortable for a while longer. We had paid off all debt in preparation for the move to Wilmington. Justin was very talented and we wanted to help him with his musical endeavors as much as we could. This is something that we knew we would never regret, spending time with both of our sons in such an unusual way. After a couple of years playing with Justin and the band, Terry thought that he needed to get back to work and bring in a regular income. After contacting a previous business associate he was able to find employment as a manufacturer's representative fairly quickly. Terry continues in this same job today. Justin continues playing music, composing music, writing songs and singing. He also teaches guitar lessons. Jeremy remains the drummer and backup vocalist. The name of Justin's band is Medusa Stone. He is married to Lauren. They have one son.

Terry and I lived in Wilmington for approximately nine years and enjoyed all it had to offer. Our extended family was nearby and that is what made it feel like home. We got together often, having dinner and cooking out. We loved the beaches, the river and the fresh seafood. Terry often caught and prepared our dinner from his fresh catches. We spent many days and afternoons on local Masonboro Island with our family and friends, walking on the island, feeling the breeze, wading in the water, watching nature, collecting shells, just having a good time with each other and the boys. Terry and I would take Casey and Justin and a friend or two wake boarding on many sun filled afternoons. Casey was most at home in any water, pool or ocean. He would always have a big smile on his face if he was in the water. He could spend hours and hours in the water. Water seemed to always bring out the best in him. Life was good and the years passed quickly as we watched our sons growing up.

Over the years we were in Wilmington, we purchased several houses. In 2006 we purchased a house in a neighborhood on the intracoastal water way. It was something we had wanted for a long time. We bought this house thinking that it was going to be our retirement home, our last move. At that time, we had seven rental houses and had just sold one of the houses for a nice little profit. We felt like we were playing real life monopoly and we thought we were on top of our game. We were not wealthy by any means, but we were comfortable. We constantly kept an eye on our credit score and guarded it like it was gold and then one day it all disappeared, the cash flow, the houses and the credit score. We happened to be in the perfect storm for a financial tragedy. It happened swiftly. Once it began it was a free fall. Loans that were prepared and discussed with the mortgage broker went awry. Our mortgage broker, Bryan was someone we had grown to trust and thought of him as a friend. We felt betrayed by his actions. He was supposed to do a personal lease/purchase with one of our homes, when it came close to the time for him to move in; he said he could not afford it. We were not prepared to hear those words. We had held the house for him to move in at a certain date. He had let us down not once, but twice. Two tenants stopped paying rent and had to be evicted. One of the tenants that were evicted opened a credit card in my name, charging several purchases. I found this out when I received a call asking me about my late payment, as I listened to the person on the other end of the phone I realized I did not recognize the bank, nor the card she mentioned, I realized that I did not have an account with them. We went to the police department immediately and told them what had happened, it was identity theft. We explained the situation and told them we knew who had opened the account. We related that she had been a tenant. She had used my social security number to open a credit card account. We think that she opened some of my mail that had gone to the old address and got my social security number from the Social Security Administration's statements that were mailed. We told the police what her new address was and where she lived, but that did not matter. They had to follow protocol and sent someone out to her old address, which was our rental property, knowing full well she no longer lived there. I thought it was a waste of our time and a waste of time and money for the police department to send someone out to an address, knowing the perpetrator did not live there. It seemed so ridiculous. I was angry about the police playing these silly games. Needless to say, nothing was ever done about it. I called the credit card company and explained she had been a tenant and she was angry about being evicted. The credit card was cancelled. I thought credit card theft was punishable by law, but the law did not care. Those commercials about credit protection make a lot of money, yes?

With several tenants not paying and evicted, our cash flow dried up as the real estate market took its first big dive. We sold two of the houses in short sales, one was sold in a mortgage transfer, and two went to foreclosure, one of them being our retirement home. We, all of us, especially Terry, had worked really hard remodeling, updating and finishing the addition of two bedrooms in the attic space. Justin and Casey had also worked hard helping us on the house. We could not have completed the work without their help. It was a family affair.

It seemed everything that could have gone wrong, did go wrong. We were tired, shocked, angry, and humiliated. It was like the knockout punch from nowhere and we were down for the count. All we could do was lick our wounds, tuck our tail and move on. Needless to say, anger had a large part in our lives over the next several months. We were just angry. Who were we angry at? It was not one particular thing that had happened. It was multiple things that happened, all of which were out of our control. Myself, my husband, as well as Justin and Casey felt devastated. We just wanted to know why. We took it all, personally. The word happy was not part of our vocabulary at that time. There was lots of confusion, stress and anxiety.

Aside from the anger, I felt like a criminal. I felt ashamed. I felt like I was less than, I felt like I didn't belong. I guess you could say I felt like an outcast. It was all self-imposed; no one had said anything to make me feel the way I did. I felt as if I had a knife in my back, a deep pain in my shoulder blade from the stress and tension I was holding in my body. The pain was constant. It was very painful.

We put the house on the market to be sold as we prepared to move out. We were doomed either way, foreclosure or not. We were not familiar with the foreclosure process and really were not sure what to do, how to do it, or where to go. I was scared, to put it simply. I wanted to run and hide, to put my head in the sand, but where could I run to? I was also exhausted from the move, from working on the house and from trying to refinance the loan. Over and over I completed paper work and more paper work. In the end, I would hear the same story about the house had lost market value. I found loans, but there was always some obstacle. I felt so overwhelmed and there was nothing I could do to change the situation, no matter how hard I tried. I was paddling up stream, against the current and I was so tired of all that paddling. We thought it would be easier to abandon ship, since we already knew that it was just a matter of time before it sank. We moved out of the house and found a house to rent. I thought finding a house to rent would provide us with some stability.

The house we found to rent had a very nice pool with a diving board, a nice yard with fruit trees and flowers and a convenient location. The house was old and ugly, tired and neglected. It had carpet in the bedrooms that was old and dirty. The walls were the ugly pink beige from my childhood memories. It appeared that little to nothing had been done to update this house in thirty years. Remember, we had all just worked our butts off for the past year, doing most of the work ourselves, renovating and remodeling a house that we thought we were going to be in for a long time. It was beautiful, comfortable and clean. We were very happy with it and felt a sense of pride for all the work we had accomplished. Moving again was not something we were looking forward to, especially to this old ugly house. I already knew that according to statistics, moving is next to divorce as one of the major stressors in life. We had a quadruple stressor going on. There was indeed a lot of stress being felt. We moved from our house in September, 2008. Our worries were not over though; during that first adjustment period when we were free falling financially we tried to refinance our vehicles. That was not going to happen either. We decided we had to return them to the bank; we could no longer pay for them. We had fallout from our credit score on many different levels. First the house insurance was cancelled on each house, next the auto insurance was going to be cancelled, even though Terry and I both had perfect driving records. We were treated like criminals, our credit score said it all. We knew we had just bankrupted ourselves and would be in our own "debtor's prison" for many years to come. Looking back on it now, it is a freedom not to have someone deciding our fate on a number; a number that indicates whether we are worthy of credit or not. No, we cannot borrow money. Sometimes it would be nice to be able to borrow money, but we are doing fine. We have no credit, we have no credit cards. We have adjusted to a new way of life, financially. We just pay as we go.

Casey's Temperament

L ife goes on. Casey, the youngest son had been acting out and having some anger issues of his own before the move from our retirement house. I attributed his increased anger to teenage hormones and stress. He was always our emotional child, but as a child I could rub his back or stroke his hair until he felt better. As he grew into his teenage years this was no longer the solution although he still liked to have his back rubbed. Before our move Casey had just learned from the high school guidance counselor that the school was not going to honor his credits for being a junior. He was missing a science credit. They were going to put him back into sophomore status. This was devastating for Casey from his point of view.

Since Casey was in the fourth grade I had him in and out of public school. We would do home school until he could stand it no longer. He was picked on by his friends for being home schooled and so he would start the new school year in the public school system. It was during the fourth grade that the teacher advised me to have him tested for ADD/ADHD; although it was not really a test, but rather an opinion. He was placed on Ritalin to aid in his focus and concentration. He had been on the pills for about two weeks when he came home and told me he told God he wished he was dead. I was horrified. I could not imagine what could have or would have made him feel this way. I asked what had happened that he wished to be dead and he told me he no longer had any friends that he just sat and ate his lunch and did his work. I called the school and asked them to throw the pills away. When I later called his teacher to inquire about his progress, this is what she said: "At least he is happy." He was not going to conform to the school environment. He was smart enough, but he would forget his pencil, forget his homework, not do the math homework showing his work when he could do it in his head. He walked to the beat of his own drummer. It was the social side of school that he wanted. He would see injustices in the school, the treatment of the special needs students by the other kids and it bothered him. He took on the woes of the world and they would bring him down like a ton of bricks. He felt everyone's emotions, the pain he perceived them to have and he would take these emotions upon himself.

I know now that Casey was an empath, one who feels the energy and emotions of others. This can be a burden or a gift. AT the time I was not aware of his ability. I knew that he was very sensitive and was always that way from birth. He felt emotions like shock waves and sometimes he could not handle them. He did not understand the feelings he was having, nor did I.

When Casey was in middle school, the seventh grade to be exact, he came home and told me his teacher was prejudice. I asked him what he meant. He said she was a black teacher and she did not like him because he was white. I told him I was sorry and that I would talk with her. When I went to the parent teacher conference the teacher told me that Casey was prejudice, She said he didn't like her because she was black. I told her I was sorry and that I would talk to him. I knew that I was being put in the middle of their personal war. I didn't think either of them were prejudice. I said nothing to either one of them. I knew this was something they would have to figure out on their own. I did have to snicker about this to myself, but I kept my laughter contained. Casey passed his grade that year by the skin of his teeth. When we went to the eighth grade open house in the fall, his old seventh grade teacher was there. They smiled and hugged each other like old friends. I had to laugh to myself at these "Two peas in a pod". I guess they had each made their peace with one another. They were a lot alike.

Casey was an extraordinary person. He always had lots of friends, from lots of backgrounds, rich or poor, red, yellow, black or white, old or young. It did not matter. He was always someone everyone wanted to be around. His smile and presence could warm a room. His blue eyes seemed to look right through you to your soul. His quiet demeanor was soothing, but if someone were out of line he did not hesitate to step in. He could say so much to you without saying a word. No one could possibly know the emotions that he allowed his family to see, his pain and hurt, the feelings and emotions that brought him down. He would maintain his composure while with friends and would let all of the emotion out at home. Once I had asked him about why he would wait until after school and explode on me when he came home. This was his answer: "Mom, I know you will love me no matter what." When he would become so upset I could not talk to or reason with him, I would write to him and slip it under his door. In giving him the letters in that manner I knew he could read it on his own time, when he was not upset.

My Dear Casey,

I want you to Know how precious you are to me and daddy.

When I said you were stubborn, I implied that it wasn't a good thing. I want you to Know something.

You have Choices to make and these choices have "ripples effects" Kind of like a rock thrown into water. The ripple affects things around it, so do the choices you make.

God has given you very special gifts and your stubborness can be used for your best interests. Once you make up your mind to do something it is that stubborness that will help you see it through to completion. It is a tool, used in the right way, a very good trait to possess.

We love you, always

Mom

He once asked me how I could be angry and "yelling" at him one moment and answer the phone so kind and sweet the next moment. I laughed and said because I am not angry at the person on the phone, I guess. He had such an unusual way of seeing things sometimes. He always thought he could do anything his brother could do, although his brother was six years older. I tried to explain it to him so that he could understand. I asked him, did a two year old get to do what he did as an eight year old? "No, of course not" he replied.

I felt responsible for Casey's happiness. Casey was my challenge, I had to be on my toes to understand where he was coming from, what he was thinking/feeling that was making him sad. He was so quiet. He was a person of very few words. When Casey was thirteen and Justin was twenty-one, I wrote them each a letter. I wanted them each to know how much I loved them and how proud I was of them as my sons. It was always my wish that they be happy in life. I wanted them to know my feelings for them, to have them in writing in case anything ever happened to me and I did not get to say the things I wanted to tell them the feelings and thoughts that were in my heart. I wanted to be sure that my boys knew how much I loved them and how proud I was and am of them.

Our situation, losing the houses and having to move yet another time just seemed to make matters worse for Casey. Fists were put into the wall upon several occasions, his anger and rage appearing from out of nowhere. The air was thick with tension. We were all feeling it and it did not feel good. It was like we were caged animals with no way out. Both of our sons felt bad for us and could not understand why all of this had to happen to their parents.

It seemed like there was an incident with Casey every other day or so as his anger seemed to turn into rage at times. We were always a close family and this hurt all of us. I knew it hurt him to hurt us in such a way. We had become a family I did not know or recognize. I knew I had to do something to help my son, to help us as a family. We just had to love Casey and help him through whatever was going on. I felt if I could get him to the age of eighteen, he would be OK. I had to find answers.

Urgings of Spirit

~≈❊❊≈~

By December of 2008 I told my family that I was getting strong urgings to deepen my knowledge about spirit, (God) about our creator. I listened to my inner voice. I dove in and began reading every book about spirit (God) I could get my hands on. I felt like I was being propelled to read, to know more of spirit. I felt like I was back in college with books everywhere. I read three or four books constantly every day. The feelings were so strong in me. I could not help myself but to do this. For all that had happened to us, I knew that I was, and we were, the same people we were before losing everything. So why did I feel so bad? Why did all of us feel so bad? Why did it have to happen this way? We had no control over the circumstances as they happened one after the other. What had I done to cause this to happen? I knew that all of this had happened for a reason and I wanted to know what that reason was. I never believed in God punishing anyone. I always felt God is LOVE. I wanted to know God better.

I searched high and low and for what, I was uncertain. As I continued to read day after day, I found myself beginning to feel some release from the stress I had been having. As I read certain information I began to have cold chills go through me. I was reminded over and over again that our Western society has placed much importance on wealth and material possessions. We placed judgment on people for the material possessions that they own or did not own. Our society treats Hollywood as if it were the home of the gods. How much money is made selling information about the rich and how they live, what they eat, who they sleep with, who they marry and who is in rehab? We seemed to give royalty and wealth a status above all others. All of their hoopla and drama sell lots of stories. Although I was never wealthy, on some level I too had bought into this same way of living without even thinking or realizing I had. I was one of the sheep, as I call it, just following along, conforming. Wealth was something we all think we want because we think it will make us happy. We collect things in our society. There is nothing wrong with money; it is just our society's perspective of it. The television, the radio, the newspapers, the internet are all selling something to us, telling us how everyone wants, needs or has to have this or that and making us think that everyone else already has it! "Why don't you?" The brainwashing is constant, relentless. We are continually bombarded with sales pitches.

As I read, I was reminded to look back into childhood again, to my favorite person, my grandma. She was such a loving, kind and gentle person. She was so good to me and I felt her love, like a warm and comfy blanket around me. Looking back now, I realize my grandma lived a very simple life. She had a one bedroom house and a bathroom was added during my childhood. She was a happy person despite her impoverished circumstances all her life. The small house and little to no furnishings did not affect my love for her or her love for me in any way. I remember she was always singing a song, "I got that joy, joy, joy, joy, down in my heart". She really did. As a child I saw her joy. I felt her joy. She had a sense of humor too. I remember she laughed quite a bit. She was someone I adored and loved to be around. You would never know she barely had two pennies to rub together. She lived on faith.

As my world and the world of my family continued to feel like it was falling apart I had to find something to hang on to, something that could give me answers, a way for us to understand what had happened to us and why. I prayed each night that I could find a way to help us to understand what had happened. As I continued to read I was reminded of what really is important in this life and that is LOVE. Love is all there is. Sound familiar? Our financial status is of little importance when compared to REAL LOVE and TRUTH. I began to realize that I was being lead and assisted in ways beyond this physical world. My heart was touched so deeply. I would read with tears in my eyes much of the time; the knowledge just seemed to be touching my heart in such a profound way. I realized that I was remembering why I had come into this life. I shared what I was learning with my family each day. Casey would call it my spiritual hoo ha. He said, "Mom I want to hear about it but, don't talk about it in front of my friends, please". I agreed not to "embarrass" him.

I was raised in the Baptist Church and had left the church at the age of eighteen. The answers I was seeking were not to be found in organized religion. As a child I would leave the church feeling low, thinking I was a sinner and would always be a sinner. I felt like I had betrayed God, but what had I done to feel that way? I was taught to believe that God was in heaven and to fear his judgment, to repent. If I didn't want to repent there would be hell waiting for me at death. It was very difficult for me to find my way into understanding God as I had been taught. As I raised my sons, they were not brought up in the church, but they were brought up knowing of our creator and of love, and the natural world. They felt comfortable in talking to God anytime.

At the time, I did not know what to call what I was learning about life and the unseen world, but I liked to refer to it as Spirit Science. The church I had gone to would have me to feel guilt and to experience fear, teaching me that God was above (separate from

41

us), that we were created in his image. I remember thinking as a child that he was a really big guy up in heaven, looking down upon us. As I would later learn, I was being lead to find my truth. I came to believe and know that our creator is within, not just within us as humans but within everything, permeating every single blade of grass, every tree, every flower, every animal, every molecule with the light and love of creation. There is no judgment by our Mother/Father Creator. We are the ones who are placing judgment on ourselves and others. There is no reason to have any fear of our Creator. We were created in love and light. Our lives are a beautiful gift; another way to experience the beauty of living and being. If we were supposed to be perfect, why come to the earth plane? There is no perfect life or perfect person. We are not supposed to be perfect. Fear and guilt go a long way to control people. In the Dark Ages, the church and the government were one and the same; so many beliefs were created out of fear. If our Mother/Father God did not want any of the things we consider wrong, ugly, or sinful, to be present on this Earth, these things would not be allowed. God is capable of all miracles. We are one of those miracles. In my readings I was reminded of the LOVE that our Creator is and that is the highest truth for me. It felt so good to know in my heart that we are made in God's form, I like to say we have the God gene. Mother/Father Source gave us the love that we are capable of from within our Spiritual heart. We have been made to believe that we are separate from Source but, we are not separate, the Divine spark is part of our heritage. As I said earlier, the light of our creator permeates every single thing. It is the life force that gives us our animation.

From the standpoint of looking back at the financial fall that my family and I took, I came to believe it was a spiritual intervention. This was an opportunity for me to stop and step back from everyday life and take a deeper look at my life, myself. Without this intervention I would not have been at a place to be receptive and feel the urgings of spirit calling me to know more. I would still be one of the sheep, just going along caught up in life. It is easy for us to get caught up in our everyday lives. Not everyone will have to experience this type of financial collapse to stop and step back, to examine your life, to find your truth. It was the way that Spirit had designed my awakening/remembering in this life.

Casey was always foremost in my mind and I wanted to help him in any way I could. It was not because I loved him more than Justin or that he was my youngest son, it was because he was going through a very difficult time. Justin was at a good place in his life, a very good place, Casey was not. I had begun learning about different types of meditations when I came across an absolution meditation. I thought this would be something that may help Casey and me. I relaxed and quieted my mind and then I mentally took Casey with me into this absolution meditation. It was a very comforting and freeing feeling that I had as I sat silently, breathing in and out, relaxing more and more with each breath. I had a picture in my mind of me walking out in nature, in a beautiful grassy field; in front of me was a large round structure of columns. They were very beautiful and appeared Greek in their design. As I walked into the structure I pictured Casey joining there. I asked and saw gold and purple light come into our presence. He and I then walked together further and further into the structure. There was much love between us, not just as mother and son; it was a love that was deeper than we could comprehend as humans, we both knew it would always be that way. There was nothing to forgive, there was only love. I later told him about the meditation I did. I told him that he was there with me in spirit, a part of the meditation. I explained to him that absolution was more than forgiveness; it was as if anything negative ever happened. He needed to hear those words. It was like I had put a balm onto his heart. I could see his eyes light up and he smiled that smile, knowing that everything was OK. He was carrying so much guilt and anger, but from what I did not know. He was in a dark place. I feared for him, but I did not know what I feared. He had told me that he was the evil one and Justin was the good one. I tried to reassure him, I did not see it that way. I would literally, whisper in his ear while he was sleeping or napping, telling him how much he was loved. No matter how much or how hard I tried to assist him or help him, I could only do so much. It was always up to Casey, in other words.

Losing Casey

A round mid January of 2009 I was having lunch with Justin, my older son when my cell phone rang; it was Rebecca, a friend of Casey's. She was hysterical and I could not understand her other than I understood her to say; Casey has blood running down his face and that they had been in an automobile accident. Justin immediately drove me to the hospital where we found Casey in the emergency room. He had blunt force trauma to his right eye and could not see out of it. They could do nothing but give him pain meds and have us see a specialist the next day. He was discharged that evening, throwing up as we left the hospital and all the way home. He continued to throw up after we were home and wanted to sleep. I drove him back to the hospital and stayed that night. We were in a room with an elderly man next to Casey. They had quite the conversation as Casey would go in and out of sleep. Casey held out his hand for me to take and I held his hand all night as he slept. I sat in the chair by his bed. That was the Casey that I knew. We would find out nine months later that he had a concussion.

An appointment for the eye specialist had been made by the hospital for the next morning. Casey and I were picked up by Terry and taken directly to the doctors' office without showers or even a change of clothes. In the eye specialist's office we would learn that Casey had what is called a hyphema. The doctor described what he was seeing as he looked into Casey's eye with his medical instrument. Casey's pupil was dilated and stuck to his lens. There was much trauma, swelling and blood in the back of the eye. All the doctor could do at this time was to treat his eye with steroids and antibiotics. The eye injury was painful and his eye was very sensitive to light. Casey had to wear dark glasses throughout the day so the light would not hurt his eye or injure his pupil any further. Casey's eye was so full of blood that his blue eye was now brown. We would go to the eye specialist several times per week for about six weeks. During those six weeks Casey would take off his sunglasses forgetting where he had placed them and then take anyone else's glasses that were conveniently nearby. We had to laugh. You never knew whose glasses he would have on when he came home.

The accident seemed to take yet another toll on Casey's emotional state. His life was interrupted and on hold. He could not work on his high school diploma at the college or play the video games that he enjoyed. He could not hit the speed bag that he was so fast with. I could see him slipping further and further. I was very concerned about him and made an appointment with our family doctor. The doctor told us Casey had post traumatic stress disorder and placed him on Klonopin, to take the edge off. I explained to Casey that this was only a temporary solution.

He had told us earlier about the fish bowl parties he had been to where all the kids bring pills and place them in a bowl and everyone just puts their hand in and takes a pill. We were concerned and warned him and his friends about taking any pills, especially pills that you don't even know what they are for, what they could do, the harm they could cause.

It was now March 2009, after several weeks of antibiotic eye drops and steroid drops Casey had eye surgery scheduled. The doctor was going to have to remove a gigantic cataract that had formed from the steroids. Three other corrective procedures were also scheduled. The doctor was going to surgically separate his pupil from the lens. It was my job to prepare Casey mentally for the surgery. He was scared, really scared. He told me he thought he was going to die young. He thought that maybe it would be during the surgery. I tried to reassure him, reminding him that his physician was a specialist who was very thorough and very knowledgeable. I wanted him to feel comfortable going into this surgery. We were told that Casey would have to have eye exams done routinely for the rest of his life due to the cataract surgery at such a young age.

As the time came close, within days of the surgery the surgical care unit called to tell us they needed $15,000 up front since we did not have medical insurance. What we did have was automobile insurance for the uninsured motorist, but our insurance company would not pay for anything, nor would the other drivers insurance. We had to cancel the surgery. I was angry for my son being a victim, having to postpone this very important eye surgery because of politics and money. I had tried very hard to mentally and emotionally prepare him for his surgery. This only gave Casey more time to worry, more time to imagine the worst. We quickly called our family and they came through with the money to help us and we could now reschedule Casey's eye surgery.

It was during this time that the crow would reappear in my life, making its presence known to me once again. I had become friends with the crow long ago. When I was a first grader outside, waiting for the school bus, a strange thing happened to me. A big beautiful crow landed on my head. He stayed there for a short visit and then flew off, leaving me and the four other kids with our mouths wide open. It was a big ordeal for me and I remember thinking quite surely that he had needed some of my hair, since it was the color of straw. That was over fifty years ago that the crow made me aware of his presence. From that moment on, the crow has always had a special place in my heart. So when the crow appeared in my life again I would take notice.

This time two crows came and appeared at my bedroom window in the very early morning hours. They were perched in the dogwood tree at the east side of the house. They were squawking and flapping their wings so loudly that they woke me up. I sat up in bed, and tried to shoo them away, telling them to be quite. They flew off only to land in the dogwood tree at the north bedroom window, again making all kinds of racket. Later in the morning I thought about the crows. I believed them to be informing me about something. I had an uneasy feeling. They definitely wanted to make me aware of something.

It was now spring time and I was hoping that Casey's favorite passion of surfing would be front and center on his mind. I was hoping that he would find some relief from his stress in knowing that he would be surfing soon. We were driving back from Statesville after a visit with my father when I told everyone we had been invited to my brother's Jerry's house for Easter Sunday dinner. Casey told us he would go and he was going to be happy, as I understood him to say, he was determined to be happy, despite all that was going on in his life. He was going to give a good effort to be happy. He loved family gatherings.

On Saturday April 10th, the day before Easter, he told us he was going fishing with a friend at one of the local ponds in the North Chase development. Earlier that morning before he departed, Terry and I made a quick trip down the street to the bank, as we came back home, we saw a boy we did not recognize leaving the house in a white car, but we thought little of it. Casey's friends were always coming and going. Casey had a smile on his face this morning. He seemed to be in a particularly good mood and made a special effort to give me and his dad a hug and kiss before leaving, telling us each "I love you" before departing. He was gone all day and had planned to spend the night with his friend, Jordan. I had tried calling him several times later that evening to make sure he was not going to be walking anywhere due to severe storm warnings. Larry, Jordan's father called to say he was dropping the boys off at our house to spend the night because they wanted to sleep in and he had to get up and go to work early. He told me Casey kept falling asleep and snoring. He said he would wake up and say a few words about Becca, who he was angry with at the time. I thought he must be exhausted. I was relieved to see Casey walk through the door with Jordan behind him that night. Casey offered me some of the candy he was eating as he went into the kitchen to get a drink and then he said good night as he and Jordan went upstairs for bed.

I went to bed shortly after Casey and Jordan. It was around 10:30pm. I was not sleeping that night and I kept hearing Casey snore and I knew that neither one of them usually snored. I got up later in the night to check in on him. As I placed my hand on his forehead it slipped into his hairline from perspiration. I thought he must be hot as I pulled the comforter back from his body. In the dark, I could see that he had fallen asleep in his jeans. He did not have a shirt on.

Storms had just passed through the area and it was a little muggy so I raised his window before going back to bed. I fell asleep for a short while, only to be awakened by what seemed like a nightmare. I was shaken to my core, almost trembling. I had seen clearly in my mind's eye, the Earth as the back drop and Casey was coming from it. I tried to make sense of it logically and reassured myself it was a nightmare. I told myself that I had just checked in on him and he was fine.

The next morning I arose around 7am, but did not shower until 8 or so. After getting out of the shower and dressed I walked into Casey's room, as I entered his room I saw Jordan asleep on the futon, directly in front of me. When I turned my head to the left to look at Casey I didn't want to believe what my eyes and my heart were telling me. I just couldn't let this information into my mind, my heart was already breaking. It was going to hurt so badly that I just could not allow it to be true. I saw a lifeless body that was my son, his spirit obviously gone.

How do I even begin to tell you? How do I describe what I was feeling? How do I convey the depth of sorrow that was coming at me? Again, time seemed to stand still in the moments it took me to gaze upon him, seeing and knowing that my son was dead, beyond any help that I could offer or give. I cannot even give words to the feelings of total helplessness, sadness and sorrow that I was experiencing. Even though I felt numb, I was mentally aware and looking at his body's position, without intending to do so. This is what I remember seeing. He was lying in his bed, on his back, just as he had been earlier when I had gone into his room to check on him. His eyes were shut; his right hand was open, palm down on his chest, over his heart to be precise. His left hand was by his side and open with the candy in it he had offered me earlier the night before. His relaxed body position told me he had gone peacefully in his sleep. I could see the blood had settled around his side and at his waist, telling me he had been gone for several hours. His usually beautiful dark skin was now a pale white. Logically, I knew he was gone and only the body was left, but I did not want to accept it in my mind. I was in complete shock and would be in shock for several days. Although I was aware and knew that my son was gone, I still had to process it somehow and let it into my world. He was my baby, my youngest son. I could not believe what my eyes were seeing and telling me. I knew in that moment that he was beyond any help

I could give him. It would take time for me to allow this horrific information into my mind. It was just too painful. My psyche was protecting me. I think that I could have gone into a million pieces, falling apart from this horrific blow of seeing my son dead. I had just checked in on him only hours before. I had just lovingly placed my hand on his forehead earlier in the wee hours of the morning. How could this be? I kept asking myself over and over. I had to absorb it slowly. I could not breathe in, nor could I breathe out. I just held my breath. Within those horrific seconds, I screamed for Terry to come upstairs. He was there within two seconds as he could hear the distress in my voice. I did not say a word as he came into the room. He looked at Casey and he too, knew immediately, that our son was gone, beyond our help. Terry put his hand over his mouth and began to sob, his pain apparent. He screamed in anger. He was angry at the world and angry that he could not help our son. He began lovingly caressing Casey's face and hair, as he too, cried in disbelief. I could not touch Casey at that time because it would just make it more real. I just did not want it to be real.

I immediately went to my cell phone and dialed 911, the operator kept telling me how to do CPR and I kept trying to tell her it was too late for CPR. I finally handed the phone to Terry and let him tell her that he was dead. I could not say the words to tell her, they would not come out of my mouth. The paramedics arrived within minutes, without sirens. They came upstairs into Casey's room, checked for a pulse and pronounced him dead. It was another blow to my psyche. It hit me like a ton of bricks as I tried to let his passing sink into another level of my mind. I felt like my heart would explode from the sadness that overcame me. I cried out in disbelief. I felt broken, shattered.

I knew I had to call Casey's brother Justin, but I did not want to tell him that his brother was gone over the phone. I told him that something was wrong with his brother and he needed to come to the house immediately. I didn't want him driving while feeling the emotions of knowing his brother was gone. Shortly afterward, Jordan had evidently called Justin without my knowledge, telling him his brother was dead. A few minutes had passed when Justin called me back. He was sobbing uncontrollably and so upset that I could not understand him. He said that Jordan told him Casey was dead. He wanted me to tell him that it wasn't true. I cannot remember what I said to him next. I could feel the hurt in his voice and I knew that his heart was breaking too. He arrived at the house shortly thereafter.

During the whole time Jordan was in Casey's room that morning, seeing, watching and hearing everything as it happened. He was not emotional. He showed no emotion on his face. He had not said a word to me or to Terry, nor had he shed any tears. He too, was in shock. I felt so bad for Jordan. I knew he was in pain for his best friend, but I also knew he would have to process Casey's passing in his own time and in his own way.

Our house was full of detectives and police officers in a very short period of time. One of the female officers asked if she could say a prayer for the family and I asked if we could include Jordan. It was about an hour or so later that I heard a blood curdling scream outside. It was Jordan. The tears and the pain he had held back earlier came forth like a river as he screamed out; "He was my best friend!"

Our house became filled with people everywhere within minutes as the news traveled throughout Wilmington like wild fire. The house was full and I felt like I couldn't breathe, if I let my breath out or even if I screamed it would all be too real. I felt like I was out of my own body and did not want to accept the truth that was before me. I was the living dead.

The only way we got through the week following Casey's death was through the love and support of our family. Over the next several days our Wilmington family, my brother, Jerry and my sister-in-law Jean, my nephews, Jason and his wife Kelly, Jeremy, and his wife Lin, all came and held us together with their love and support. Justin and his fiancé' Lauren worked those five days planning and preparing the video tribute to Casey that was to be played during the memorial service. Justin and Lauren did not leave the house, staying with us the first week after Casey's passing, never leaving for very long. Our families, all of them, were our foundation at this time. They, along with friends and caring others brought us food each day. Our house remained full night and day with friends and family for the next five days until the memorial service. When I went to bed it was from complete exhaustion. Each morning I awoke to relive what had taken place, my son was dead, gone from us. The family organized and strategized everything that needed to happen within those days prior to Casey's memorial. We were held in their love and they were our strength. They were our legs, seeing that we were taken care of in so many ways. Someone in the family was always there with us the first few days after Casey's passing and throughout the planning of his memorial service and the reception that was planned for afterwards.

Some of the family went with us to meet Reverend Elaine from the Universal Unitarian Church who would be conducting the memorial service. She wanted to know a bit about Casey, since she would be speaking about someone she did not know personally. We each told her a little piece of info about him and she came to know him very quickly. We decided that we wanted to have shells at the entrance for people to write on and say their farewells, to be placed in a basket up front. Shells seemed to be appropriate since Casey loved the ocean so much. Our friend Sandy and her son, Tenor who is our great nephew, wanted to design and make the register for the reception. Lin and Jeremy brought roses to be placed on the table by the basket of shells. We had individual candles to be lit for those who wished to say something about their memories of Casey.

The day of the memorial came so quickly and I had my sweet friend, Dawn by my side and my sister-in-law, Sherry helping me to get dressed. Our family friend Kim, was there staying by our side for several days. Again, I felt like I could not breathe and I did not want any of it to be true. I was still in shock and I was still being protected by my psyche until I could let all of this into my world a little at a time.

It was decided that my brother, Jerry would drive us to the church. Terry and I sat in the back seat. We held hands so tightly. We were both feeling the hurt and pain of letting our son go. It was a very short distance to the church and yet it felt like one of the longest trips I had ever taken. We were there a bit early and really did not plan for many people to be there. Terry and I sat down on the first pew in the middle of the church and waited for our family members to arrive.

As the service began, Reverend Elaine welcomed everyone and asked those who wished to speak to take a candle light it and then place it in the dish filled with sand. Several of Casey's friends got up and spoke about their friendship with Casey and shared some of their memories. Justin got up and said his loving words about his brother and what Casey had meant to him as his brother and his friend. Casey's Aunt Judy spoke about the young Casey she got to know. Reverend Elaine then raised her arms to motion people closer in preparation to see the video that Justin and Lauren had put together for Casey. When Terry and I turned around we were quite surprised, the whole church was full and people were standing in the aisles. The memorial was simple and perfect. As the service ended we could see many people there were young school friends of Casey's, some were people we did not know, some were people we had not seen in a long time. We saw Casey's teacher and friend, Mr. Wood.

I read all of the shells that were signed for Casey. Some I could make out and some I could not but it did not matter because I knew that Casey saw them and he read them even if I could not. Mr. Wood, his teacher wrote "One so easy to love." I cried and cried after reading it because Casey was so easy to love. I knew that he considered Mr. Wood a special friend, not just as a teacher. He confided and talked with Mr. Wood often on their rides to and from school. All of the shells had beautiful messages written on them and the shell will always remind me of Casey's love of the ocean.

The week after the memorial was probably one of the worst times for me because everyone had left and had gone back to their lives and we had to return to our lives as well, but somehow I just did not feel like I could. My heart felt like it had a big hole in it and my life had a big empty place. The house was so very quiet. I would be hit with emotion after emotion. I wanted him back so badly. I just had to feel the pain of the emotion, never knowing what may trigger a memory. It was difficult for both Terry and me as we felt the emptiness and sadness of it all.

I began writing to Casey in my journal. I "talked" with him in my journal whenever I felt the need to do so. I wrote several poems to him to honor him. It was a way for me to express myself and communicate with him in my own way. *I would watch the video that Justin and Lauren had made many, many times, remembering all those precious moments, crying each time. Justin wrote beautiful songs to his brother, expressing his love, his grief and how he felt about losing him.

The Casey One

Kind and Gentle, Loving and Free-spirited

He was these things and more

Handsome and Well-mannered

Chiseled and Toned. Tanned and Blue eyed

Compassionate and Concerned

All the things that were seen by others

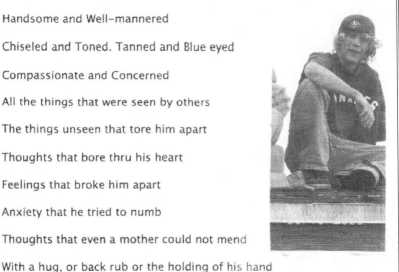

The things unseen that tore him apart

Thoughts that bore thru his heart

Feelings that broke him apart

Anxiety that he tried to numb

Thoughts that even a mother could not mend

With a hug, or back rub or the holding of his hand

Prayers were sent and prayers were answered

He is now in heaven. He is flying. He is soaring.

He is more than he thought he ever could be

For now he knows he is a child of God, held in love, perfect.

He is Happy. He is complete.

One afternoon, I was lying on the sofa about to take a nap, when I felt what I thought was one of our cats coming to lie down with me, when I looked at my feet to see which cat it was I saw no one. I knew I had felt the weight of someone and I knew that someone must be Casey. I know he was oh, so close and I had to hold that thought in my heart and my mind. I would not feel it again.

What Happened to End Casey's Life

There was still the matter of what had happened to cause Casey's death. It would be several months before we would know the cause of death from the autopsy. The police had put a picture together from the information they gathered within the week following his death. We were told that a boy down the street owed Casey some money, that he paid Casey with two timed release morphine pills. It would turn out to be the boy Terry and I had seen leaving our house that Saturday morning before Casey's death. We were also told about the depth of pill usage and barter that was going on with the teens. We were told Casey planned to sell these pills for money, but something changed and he along with two other boys crushed and snorted the pills that day. I am sure that they had not taken into consideration that by crushing a timed release pill that they were potentionaly ingesting six or more hour's worth of morphine at one time.

At no time did I ever think that Casey had deliberately taken his own life. Casey was self medicating. We are a culture of pill takers. Most all of us have taken pills for headaches, pain, depression and the list goes on. I understood he was trying to feel better. We have brought up generations and generations thinking that pills are magic. The danger and death from these new timed release morphine pills were not made public, but after talking with a retired coroner he said that the abuse and death rate from these pills alone, was exceptionally high.

After learning this boy literally lived right down the street, I had become aware that I passed his house on the way out of our neighborhood almost every day. I looked at his house like it was going to tell me something, wanting to stop and talk to him. I told myself that I needed to wait until Casey's cause of death was confirmed. Several months later we received the official notification from the state, the autopsy read: "morphine intoxication". After reading it, I had not planned to stop at their house that day, I just did. I was by myself and Terry was out of town working. I pulled into the driveway, got out of the car, walked to the front of the house and introduced myself to the stepfather who was sitting on the front porch at the time. I related the story of Casey's passing and the course of events that had happened the day of his passing as determined by the police from their questioning of Casey's friends. The step-dad told me that explained a lot and asked me to have a seat while he got the boy's mother. After a short while I was invited into the house and introduced to the boy's mother. She told me she has cancer and that was her prescription he had taken. They indicated that he had not gone to Casey's memorial, but his younger brother had gone. They had thought it to be strange. They also told me he had been very upset and had a tattoo put onto his forearm that read: R. I. P. Casey Fox. I asked if I may talk with the boy. I indicated that neither I nor my husband had blamed him for Casey's death. They indicated that would be fine if we spoke to their son, but he was not home at the time. I thanked them for their time and left for home. The mother indicated that she would bring him to our house.

It would be almost a month before we heard the knock at our front door. I opened the door; it was the boy and his mother.

I introduced myself to the boy and invited them in and we went upstairs to Casey's bedroom. We all had tears in our eyes immediately. I hugged the boy and it felt like hugging Casey. He was tall and thin like Casey. I told the boy that I did not blame him for Casey's death. I told him I wanted him not to blame himself and that I wanted him to grow old and tell his kids about his friend Casey. Terry had been down stairs in the kitchen preparing dinner. I called for him and asked if he could come up to Casey's bedroom and join us. He entered Casey's room with tears in his eyes and he too hugged this young boy and told him we did not blame him for our son's death. It was never even discussed that we had any blame or anger at this young boy what so ever. We both felt the same way about the boy.

From the very early days we had been concerned for this young man we had not met. We felt that he must have been carrying the weight of the world upon his shoulders, a burden that Terry and I wanted to help remove. We had hoped that our verbally telling this young man that we did not blame him for Casey's death would help to release him from the responsibility and guilt that he was carrying. I was not sure how much our words helped to ease his mind and lighten his burden, but we had to try.

A little over a year after Casey's passing we were told of the boy's death. Again, it seemed like another tragedy had taken place. The boy was found dead, cause of death; morphine intoxication. His mother had told us that he could not let go of the guilt he felt. She said he spoke about Casey often, although I do not think that they were close friends. It would have been a heavy burden for anyone to think that they are responsible for another's death, but especially one so young.

Looking Back

From the point of looking back, it became apparently clear that losing everything just did not matter; it was of little concern after finding our Casey gone. At that time I could have lived in a dirt hut and it would not have mattered in the least. Everything in my life had a different value assigned to it. I was letting go of the attachments I had for anything of material wealth. Whereas; before Casey's passing, before losing everything, I had a different value I had placed on material possessions, now all emphasis was being placed on the soul, knowing that I am the soul having a human experience. I was beginning to see myself from the viewpoint of the soul. I was beginning to understand some of the reasons, the lessons; I had come to learn in this life. I was learning to be the real me, not just the personality I identified myself as. I was letting go of the "life" I had been lead to believe from the mass consciousness, from family, from church, from school, from friends. I was learning to walk the sacred path and to trust myself on a much deeper level. I was beginning to know that I was much more than I ever conceived. Spirit had intervened in a way that was assisting me to prepare for something much, much bigger. I was being prepared for the death of my youngest son, but I was also being prepared to view life from another perspective. I knew this deep inside of my heart, but I was also being prepared to know that this life is part of a much, much bigger picture.

After his passing I continued to go deeper and deeper into knowing about our world from the perspective of spirit. Oh yes, I still grieved for my son. I am in no way saying that it was easy for me. My heart ached for him. I wanted him back in my world so badly. I had defined myself as Casey and Justin's mother, now that definition was fractured. I had to continue to justify and understand my place in this world. As my world continued to grow bigger and bigger each day, I came to realize the little fish bowl that most of us view life from. We don't even realize it. I would come away each day with a new understanding, one that would allow me to expand my perspectives in a most comforting and loving way. As I came to understand life in a new way, I also came to change the thoughts that create my world. By opening my mind and acknowledging myself as the soul, I was able to see and know life in a totally different way. I began to see myself as more than this personality self, as the Sherri one, the soul having a human experience. I began to see myself as worthy of knowing that I am the soul first and foremost. The Sherri self is just one of the lives and lessons I am experiencing. I was beginning to see past the illusion of this life. We are all playing our parts. I was able to see that life has no coincidences. It is all divinely orchestrated for us. It is Creator's way of seeing to it that certain things happen at certain times for the soul to experience and learn. It is an opportunity for us. Life offers us synchronicities, what we may call coincidence. These little coincidences may seem to be simple or unbelievable. They may be miraculous. Either way these events are gifts to us, just as our lives are gifts. Miracles happen every day. I could not believe that there is so much more to life than what I had been led to believe. I had been walking in the dark and now the light was coming in and allowing me to see life in a totally different way.

The night of Casey's passing, I had the vision of the earth as the backdrop and Casey coming from it; I was being gifted the knowledge of knowing when my son had left physicality, his death as we refer to it. I didn't think that I was prepared to know or accept such a gift at the time it was presented to me, but as I look back from the perspective that I now have, I feel most honored for this most beautiful of gifts. I am very thankful for this most caring acknowledgement of his life and the love that I have for him as the "Mother One" of the "Casey One". In other words I was most lovingly being prepared in a way that was not in words at all but as an image, one that I had to discern the meaning of for myself. To me it was very apparent what this image represented, his death from this life. When the image was presented to me at the time of his death I did not have any reference points in which to place the significance of its meaning because I was using the logical side of my brain and thinking it through. If I could have just allowed and accepted this image, I would have known immediately, what I was being shown. The way that my body reacted and felt as the image was being viewed was quite different from my logical reaction. My body felt shaken to the core. My body reacted before my brain. The body, the heart, and the right side of our brain are the most intuitive parts of our being. They do not have to have evidence to support their reaction, the knowledge just is. We have forgotten how to use our true gut reactions without using our logical brain to analyze everything.

I have told you the story of losing my youngest son and the perspectives that I had at the time of his passing and how those perspectives changed. For all of Casey's life I was trying to help him to cope with feelings and emotions he did not understand. The night of his passing I thought he was safe at home asleep in his bed. I was trying to control life. I was operating out of the logical side of my brain. I had not been living through the heart; the spiritual heart will never lie. It is always true. There were so many thoughts about Casey's death that I had to let go of. I kept thinking if only I had done this or if only I had done that. I wanted to place blame on myself for his death, but it was out of my hands. It always was. I had come to realize that our lives are always Divinely orchestrated. I had also come to understand that all is as it should be and all is as it should have been as my friend Toni has reminded me. I cannot emphasize this statement enough. God, our creator is the one in control. We're here to experience and learn!

Although, neither Casey nor I knew on a conscious level what was going to happen, we were both feeling what was to happen and take place. Casey had a bit of a quick life before leaving. He came into this life ready to leave. He had several exit points available to him before he was born. He could have chosen to take his leave at any of those times. I went into pre term labor with Casey many times until I was put on complete bed rest and given a drug called Breatheine. This drug was used to relax the uterine muscle and keep me from contracting. It is a drug that is used for asthma patients, to relax the chest muscles. Although the drug that was prescribed did what is was supposed to, it was still out of my control. It is always in the hands of our creator. We have to be able to look at the big picture of our many lives; Remember, we are here to experience and to learn. While on the other side, the unseen world to us, we are in our creators love and light. We know the truth of things. I really do not think that I could have foreseen the great emotional pain that I would have, perceiving the passing of my son as a loss. Experience is the greatest teacher.

Many have called me brave and strong but I do not think or feel that I am either for accepting the passing of my son. I accept his passing because I know that we are eternal. I WILL SEE HIM AGAIN. How can I continue to be sad, to cry for my son who had gone back home and is in our creators love and light. It is a feeling, a belief that is so true, so propelling for me that it is my truth. I know deep in my heart that this life and any life on any planet, in this existence is part of the All That Is. We are all involved in this beautiful dance with life. It is up to us to realize we are a partner in this dance.

I kept having the thought, the feeling, if I could only get Casey to eighteen years old, he would be fine. I didn't realize why I kept having those thoughts and feelings until his passing. Then it all became so clear. I was not meant to know this consciously, how could I have experienced it as I did, had I known? I came to understand that we are here to learn, to experience for creator and to expand the knowledge and experience of our soul. We are the soul. We are eternal. We are Divine beings at our very core, all of us. I have not lost him, I perceived it as loss. He exists in another way. What I may see as loss is illusion. This life is merely a focused intent. I have come to understand that linear time is also part of the illusion, all time exists now. The best analogy I have found to explain it is this; consider that all of our lives were on a big, huge canvas and it is so big that we cannot see all of it at once. We have to focus on certain areas. We, in this life are merely one facet of the many lives that our soul is living. We leap frog in and out of lives, coming and going and if I really believe this as my truth, how can I have any sadness for Casey because he went back into total alignment with source, remembering all that he is, was and ever has been. Love, real love, not the emotional, ooey, gooey stuff we call love, is and has to be the answer.

I have a little story that I came across. I think it was meant as a way to explain death to our little ones, but it works for me just fine.

As a way to further explain and understand death, I have written a poem that was inspired by the author of the poem "Water Bugs and Dragonflies", Ms Doris Stickney. In this analogy of death we are given greater insight and understanding of what death is. We can allow and suspend our judgment of death and "see" it as another way of being.

Nymphs and Mayflies

In the bottom of our little pond lives a group of water bugs or nymphs as they are called. They live a happy little life together in the water. For this reason, they could not understand why none of them ever came back home after going to the surface of the water.

After quite the discussion they got together and promised each other that the next one that left for the water's surface must promise to return and tell the others about what happened.

It was not long until one of the group felt the urge to depart for the surface, remembering full well his promise to the others. He found himself lying on the surface of the water. In the process of immerging from the water's surface he went through a transformation. As he gazed upon himself he saw that he was now a beautiful mayfly with wings!

Remembering his promise to his friends, try as he may to enter the water, he could not. He flew round and round and back and forth, but he could not enter the water. He felt sad and bewildered for a moment and then he realized that even if his friends saw him now they would not recognize him. He decided he would just have to wait for them to come join him.

He flew off into his beautiful new surroundings joyously looking forward to his next wondrous journey.

WE matter! WE matter! All of us matter. Not just some, but all. Some are lost in the illusion, but that is OK. Some of us feel separate from our Source. There may be feelings of homesickness for some. Life may appear not worth living. You may know someone that fits this description. All we can do is reassure them, let them know of their worth. Let them know you understand their pain. Accept them as they are. As I have said, we are all on different paths, all leading back to the same destination.

Although it did take time, patience and allowance, one by one I let go of all of my feelings of guilt, of trying to define the reason for his passing. I would have such profound lucid dreams after his death. There would be dreams of his coming back and within the dream would come the clarity of why this was not going to happen. I was being allowed to live in those dreams and feel what I wanted so badly, to have him back. Logically, I knew he could not come back to this world as the Casey One, but from an emotional stand point as his mother, I wanted him back, oh, how I wanted him back! I imagine while on the other side I saw this as something I could do with ease, because I knew what the real deal was, but once here in the human form, the veil is down and amnesia sets in.

It took time for the grieving process. Emotions would come in waves and then they would ebb. I could be hit from out of nowhere and have to excuse myself. I continued to remain on my spiritual path as it was my only way of finding the depth of understanding that I needed, to accept what I considered as a tragic loss at the time.

Moving Forward

〜ℰ ℋ〜

E
arlier before Casey's passing I had asked him if he would go and talk with a spiritual counselor, thinking that maybe he would be more open with someone he did not know. He agreed that he would go. The day came for the appointment and he had changed his mind, he would not go. I had to call Elaine and cancel. I apologized for the inconvenience. After his passing it would be me that would go to see Elaine, the spiritual counselor. She was going to do a past life regression with me which involved being hypnotized. I was so excited to get to experience this. We talked for a while and I felt very comfortable with Elaine, she was very understanding and soft spoken. As we began, she had worked on relaxing me deeper and deeper, but as she continued I had to stop her, I realized I would not allow myself to be hypnotized. I would not relinquish control. I did return to see her however; for another session, but this time I asked her if she would do an Angel Reading for me. In an Angel Reading the thoughts, feelings and images are received from the other side and are related to the client. During the session I had been wearing an eye mask so as to be in complete darkness. As Elaine began telling me what she was seeing and feeling in her mind's eye, tears began to run down my cheeks. What she was telling me was so beautiful and touching

and being applied directly to my heart. The love that I felt was overwhelming and all I could do was cry. Elaine is a very beautiful person, someone I had just met and felt like I had known her all my life, perhaps I did in another life.

After our session I told Elaine I would like to have a Reiki Attunement. I would define an attunement as one having the intent to pass on certain knowledge and or abilities to another. She indicated she no longer gave attunements, but gave me the name and number of someone she thought I would really like. I felt myself turning red with embarrassment. What I had meant to say is that I wanted to make an appointment for a Reiki session. What came out of my mouth was; I wanted a Reiki Attunement. I did not even know what an attunement was. I just had to realize that spirit was working through me and trust the process.

After I got home I told my husband what I had said to Elaine about an attunement and then I went into the house and I called the number Elaine had given me. The Reiki instructors name was Pat. I left a message on her answering machine for her to call me about taking Reiki. After leaving the message, I thought to myself, she sounds like a regular person, an everyday woman. I don't know what I was expecting her to sound like. I had placed some kind of an expectation out there. I guess I thought she was supposed to sound Angelic or something. Sometimes I just have to laugh at myself and my expectations. She called back within the hour. She was very polite and gave me the cost for the Reiki I class certification and the date for our first class session.

I was very excited about this Reiki class even though I was still grieving the loss of my Casey. I thought this would be a continuation of my learning. I had taught myself a little about the chakras (our spiritual energy centers) a few years back. I had been very interested in knowing more. The day of the class came and we met at Pat's house. It was an all day event. Pat had prepared a wonderful lunch for all of us. There were six women in my class, all of us taking Reiki I and all of us from very different backgrounds, religions and beliefs. We began the class with each of us introducing ourselves. After our introductions we got down to the business of our initiation, our attunement. Pat put a certain essential oil on our palms and said words I did not understand. She made symbols with her hand and then she gave me the name of a country and indicated it was where I had done my most intensive healing work in a past life. She also told each one of us about our Reiki Master on the other side. She took each of us, one at a time and did a certain ritual and said certain words. She told our class that "they" had told her that one would be a great healer and another, would tone. (One who heals through using the voice to tone certain musical notes.) I didn't think I would be the one toning because I could not hold a tune. I kept wondering who (they) were. After our first Saturday class we would meet every Tuesday night at Pat's house for eight weeks. She gave us notebooks filled with our curriculum. We learned the history of Reiki and how it came about, what Reiki was. We learned about energy; how to feel energy. We learned how to use a dowsing pendulum. Dowsing is the same principle that was accepted and used not so long ago, to locate water underground using the forked limb of a willow tree. We learned about the chakras, their location in the body and their respective colors. We learned that the chakras correlate with the colors in the rainbow. To remember those colors Pat taught us this little acronym; ROY G BIV; red, orange, yellow, green, blue, indigo and violet. Pat taught us a little about crystals and the vibrations that they have and how the color of the crystal assists in healing as well. Pat always had homework for us to do and practice exercises to work on before we would return for the next class.

During and before I started the Reiki class I had been asking for a sign, praying for a sign from above that I was on the right trail, that I was doing what I needed to be doing. I was still a closed minded skeptic when it came to myself. One evening on the way to my Reiki class, I was stopped at a red light and the van to my right was turning right. As the van pulled out and was making his turn to the right, what I read in big bold letters was; "A Sign From Above" I read those words and I just laughed out loud. (They), my angels, guides, those on the other side, had to put something right there before my face so I could see it and not doubt it. It was like they said, can you see this Sherri? It wasn't that I didn't take it seriously. I was laughing at myself. I had to laugh at myself. I was so doubtful, so unsure of myself. I did not trust myself. That evening I told the class about the sign on the van and they too thought it was funny. Pat reminded us that it was still a sign and we all agreed. Remember there are no coincidences.

My Reiki class was something that I looked forward to each week. I was learning so much and I was drinking in every ounce of this beautiful information. All of the women in my class were so sweet, so compassionate and caring with me as they were told about my son's passing. It was a most wonderful place for me to continue healing from my grief. Pat was the perfect teacher for me. She is far more than a Reiki Master; she is a Master Teacher, offering those who are ready, a chance to delve into the knowledge of spirit and life on the other side. We were learning so much more than Reiki. We were being initiated into the unseen world. I began to see clearly just what an active place the unseen world was. It did not matter that I didn't see it with my eyes. I could feel it with my heart. I was beginning to see my world through the perspective of the soul. Pat taught us the soul mantra, which is a good way to acknowledge ourselves as the soul. It is a mantra that I like to say each day at least once, but as often as needed to remind myself that I am the soul first and foremost.

The Soul Mantra

I am the soul.
I am the Light Divine.
I am love.
I am will.
I am fixed design.

This mantra teaches and reminds us that we are the soul, made in the image of our maker, the Light Divine. It reminds us that we are love, as that is what our creator is. The mantra also reminds us that we are will, God's will. We are fixed design reflects the fact that we are here to fulfill a mission, our contract, so to speak. We have a purpose for being here. As we say the soul mantra, we are letting the soul know that we recognize it and are asking for engagement, that we are worth engagement. We know that we are more than our personality self and that our bodies are our vessels. We are then able to see past the illusion of this life.

Pat, my Reiki instructor had been a school teacher for all her life and now she was teaching something quite different from the regular school curriculum. With each of our classes we would learn something new about spirit, about ourselves and Reiki. As we went deeper into our Reiki teachings Pat had each of us, one by one to lie upon the massage table while the rest of the class practiced working with energy as she stood with us, instructing us, one by one. At first I felt nothing and then I began to sense and know where I needed to place my hands on the person. I began to sense and feel when spirit would come into the room or be present.

We were learning about energy and how to trust our guts and work to initiate healing through this beautiful energy. I think the most beautiful thing that I learned and appreciate is the prayer that we were taught to say before each session. Pat taught us to always ground ourselves with Mother Earth first, to always ask permission of the client to do Reiki before going any further. Pat would have us to set our intent to be a clear channel for Reiki's healing energy. In our prayer we ask for the highest and best for the client. I thought this was appropriate for any prayer for often we ask for what we think is best or what we want to happen. Often what we pray for may not be in the highest interest of the soul. Pat taught us to always ask for the angels to be present. We also ask that the guides and angels of the individual be present, as well as our Reiki Master. We ask for any messages that were to be passed on to the client. Pat always reminded us that we were just a channel for the energy, God's energy, to pass through us and to the client. Pat has a saying that I love to hear. She says as she shrugs her shoulders, "I just work here".

With Pat's assistance, love and tenderness, her past life readings, and Reiki sessions, as well as the support, love and friendship of the group, I began to heal and to understand life on a deeper level. I began to understand and learn things about myself and the unseen world that I did not know consciously. I continued Reiki with Pat for over a year, eventually becoming a Reiki Master. I came to love Pat as a dear friend and mentor. I am most grateful for being placed in her loving hands. Within that year of being loved, nurtured and healed I began to find my strength again. Not only did I find my strength, I felt like the Albatross, I had risen from the ashes to begin life anew. I had found my inner light, my worthiness. Although the inner light was always within, as it is with all of us, I was now beginning to honor myself and all life with new eyes, new perspectives. I was understanding life on a new level.

It has been almost four years since the passing of my youngest son. I often refer to him as "The Casey One" because this reminds me that he did not come here for me, but through me. His soul had its own agenda, no matter how painful I perceived his passing to be.

I have mentioned this earlier, but I have had people to tell me how strong I am. I must admit, that I have wondered, pondered what that means. For if I am strong, it is only because of the faith that I have in my heart and the belief that love is our truest quest. Meredith Murphy talks about our courage in her quote that follows: "Remembering our True Divine Nature takes courage. For it's not simply an idea, it's a realization-and when you become aware of something as fact, you then live from its knowing." WE are God in form in this 3rd dimension. I have come to understand and see my truth as only I perceive it to be, but that does not mean it is right or it is wrong, it just is. I have come to see that we are truly all equal in all ways. It is our perception of life that creates our reality.

Shortly after Casey's passing we had gone to visit relatives and I had let the fear of thinking he was gone, dead, come over me, it was only for a multi second but, I truly felt like I was falling from a tight rope way up high or walking in quick sand that was about to take me under. It was a very scary feeling even for those short little seconds. I made the choice in those few moments of fear to know in my heart that life is truly eternal, to always remind myself of my True Divine Nature. This is not the end. I will see him again. He is always in my heart. What feels like a long time for us here in the 3rd dimension in this life is more like a quick passing when you view life from an eternal point of reference.

Although I miss Casey each day, what I had perceived as loss has been replaced with the deeper knowing that his life as "The Casey One" is over and he exists in another way. I now know with much love and acceptance in my heart, that my Casey had come into this life for certain situations and learning and that he knew (although unconsciously) when this life was over he would drop his physical body and return home for a duration, being, existing, in another way. I say duration because we don't just go home to heaven and sit and twiddle our thumbs, no, there is always something to learn, a new experience to be had, a different dimension to experience it from. Our creator allows all of us to experience many, many, many different learning scenarios. We all understand that there is no teacher like the teacher of experience. To feel and experience something firsthand is the ultimate learning experience. Although we view ourselves from our personality stand point, it is just part of the "prop" we are using for this life. We have had many personalities, many vessels and we have been from different races, backgrounds and planets. We hale from many different planets. We have been both male and female. We have loved many and many have loved us. Allow yourself to feel this, don't analyze it logically. It is all good. Source energy is in everything throughout the omniverse. I say omniverse which is bigger than the universe, because I believe there is so much more for us to know, to remember. This is just one of the worlds that is available to us.

For me, I know that the ending of this life is not the end. It never is. I hold Casey in my heart and he is only a thought away. I will see him again. "All the world's a Stage . . . And all the men and women are merely players." I know that our love is eternal. We did not stop loving each other at his passing from this earth, just as your loved ones and you will not stop loving one another.

I think that Casey and I both knew on another level of our being, what was about to take place, although we were not consciously aware. I think that is why he thought he was going to die young and I thought I had to get him to eighteen years of age. He passed on April 11, 2009. He would have been eighteen on his birthday, May 28, 2009. I thought he would be at a "safe" place in his life. We were both playing our parts and finding what real love was and is, while we were doing it. Casey is still teaching me about life as I reflect on the many words that passed between us, the interaction of our lives together, the love that we had for one another and the love of our family. He is forever a part of me. I am forever a part of him. He is forever in my heart. WE are all a part of each other.

If I could say anything to you about life, about death, it is this. Know that the ones who have passed are merely gone from our sight. We all have loved ones on the other side who care about us and love us, who, along with others are assisting us with our life events. We all may have situations to happen in our lives that seem to take us into our own personal hell, but we can get past these situations and rise above them. We can move beyond those conditions and move forward in life. I want you to know that this is a beautiful world in which we live. I want you to feel it and know it in your heart. I want you to know just how precious, how wonderful, how beautiful you are in the eyes of creator. I hope, after reading my story that you will allow yourself the freedom to find your truth, to know that this life is just part of the focused intent of illusion we are experiencing. Time is malleable and pliable. I will say it again, time is malleable and pliable. There is no time on the other side. We experience linear time in our reality. It is all good.

We will all have life situations that are challenging; some may appear more tragic or sad. Remember we are not defined by our situations. We are the soul. We are all on different paths, but traveling to the same destination. I want you to know that you are loved more than you realize and that we are all connected, just like drops of water in the ocean, those drops seeming separate, but part of the whole. We only see ourselves as separate.

We are part of a beautiful web of love and light that connects all of creation. It is this connection that plays in and out of our life in such subtle ways that we may not even notice. We live in a magical world. Miracles do happen every day! We are all being informed of life on many different levels, ways that do not intrude or startle, in ways too many to imagine. All we have to do is tune in and allow. I do not pretend to have all the answers; in fact, the more I learn, the more I realize what I do not know and that is OK. We don't have to know all the answers. We just have to be, to allow. If you can take one thing away from my story that may assist you on your path in life, I will be much honored.

Life happens and it is our response to those circumstances that will determine the directions we will go next. It is up to you and I to move forward with a lighter spirit and a more optimistic and energetic approach to life and to living. Although life may appear cruel and often harsh we can still find the opportunity to move forward, to heal and to seek that which will bring us happiness again. We must know that our creator would not allow anything to happen that is not supposed to happen. It is all as it should be. It is all as it should have been. We must look at the big picture and know life happens for a reason. It may seem that life gets in our way, but it is how we react to life that is the real answer to this question of happiness and joy. There is always help for us. All we have to do is ASK for assistance from the unseen world, listen and allow.

It seems particularly difficult on our society to lose our young ones, to lose anyone, but the lessons of the soul are many and varied, what one needs to learn in a short life may take another a lifetime. We do not always need live a long life in order to learn for the soul. The scenarios are different and varied for each of us. There is no need to fear death. When we can look at death from the perspective of acceptance and love, we can find peace in our heart. We must have faith that our loved ones are fine. Faith is the key word here. If we want proof, there is none. That is what faith is, trusting our heart without any fixed logic to support it. We must know in our hearts that our loved ones who have passed are surrounded by love, they are LOVE. They remember all when on the other side, not just this life but all of the other lives as well. Sometimes I think about others that I may have had to pass before me in other lives. I wonder about the others that I have loved as spouses, children, siblings, family, friends, and lovers. I know that we must love one another as well. In truth, to me, we are all beautiful light beings, souls that are pure love and joy. I know that I carry those memories within my very cells. It is all there stored and ready to retrieve. When we can realize that we are all family and can treat one another with love and respect, our world will change for the better in the wink of an eye. The loved ones we have to pass before us are held in the love of our mother/father God, remembering all. There is no perception of separation. Love is eternal. It does not stop because of death. I have not stopped loving Casey for one moment not before his passing and not after his passing. As I keep saying, life goes on. It is just going in a different way. There are many ways of living, of being. It is all good.

Returning Home to the Farm

lmost a year and a half after Casey's passing Terry had told me that we needed to return to Statesville, words I did not care to hear. He was pretty insistent about his decision. I agreed to go, although reluctantly. Justin was weeks away from being married. We wanted to wait until after Justin and Lauren's wedding to move back to the farm. Casey was supposed to have been Justin's best man in the wedding ceremony. He was excited to be a part of his brother's wedding. On the day of Justin's wedding, as I watched and observed the ceremony, I imagined Casey was there with us. I could see him in his tuxedo, looking so handsome and grinning with those beautiful dimples showing. I really didn't have to imagine, I know he was there. He wouldn't miss his brother's big day.

Within days after the wedding, we were packing our belongings to leave for Statesville before Justin and Lauren had left for their official honeymoon. I guess there were many reasons for our return to Statesville, but I was not happy about moving back home, four and a half hours away from our son, our new daughter-in-law, family and friends that I love. I felt like I was abandoning Justin when Casey's passing was still so fresh in his mind and in his heart. I think that Justin was in a precarious position of missing his brother and feeling so low, on one hand. On the other hand, he was marrying the girl he loved and was about to start a new life. Our move just seemed to be another low point for him.

I had to agree with Terry that moving back to the farm was the right thing to do, as my father was turning eighty nine years old and I did not want him to be alone. Financially, it was a smart thing to do, but my emotions were telling me another story. The whole Wilmington family was at the house on moving day, including Justin and Lauren. Everyone was there to help us pack and load our things into the rental truck. Moving day was a sad scene. We were all a little bummed about the move. I remember pulling out of the driveway when it was time to go and crying so hard that I could not see to drive. My heart felt like it was breaking again. I was truly overwhelmed with sadness. It was July 4th, 2010. Wilmington was hot and humid, making the packing, move and drive all the more difficult. Terry drove the rental truck and I drove the pickup truck. We did not stop for three hours. I continued to cry on and off as I allowed my thoughts of leaving to overtake my mind and my emotions to overwhelm me. I felt so sad leaving our son. Deep inside I knew Justin would be fine. He was married to a wonderful girl and had the love and care of our family and now the love and care of Lauren's very large family in Wilmington. I still felt like I was driving to hell. We did have some family in Statesville, but it had been so long since we had lived there that I felt like a stranger coming to a new town. I think my father was somewhat glad that we were returning because he could no longer manage the workload of the farm by himself. I am not so sure he was looking forward to giving up his sanctuary to me and Terry. He had always been a lone wolf.

It was a difficult move for me for many said and unsaid reasons. I would have to make the best of the situation. In the past we had tried to live with my father after my mother's passing, but we would end up leaving and moving back to Wilmington. I would leave because I could not take the negativity of my father. I would either be crying from one day to the next or angry. He could say mean things to me that cut me to the bone or he would just plane out insult me. It just did not work out. This time I had to remind myself that I was a different person, although from the outside no one could tell any difference. I could tell. I knew that I was a different person. It would still be a challenge for me. I was able to see life from a much broader perspective. As the "Sherri One" I had allowed my father to hurt my little ego. As one seeing life from the perspective of the soul I knew that my father was playing his part as the "Bob One" and I just had to love him as I had loved Casey when he was angry and acting out. Now, I knew that my father was offering me an opportunity, a lesson to be learned and experienced. It was up to me. I am the only one I can control and sometimes that is debatable. I tell my Terry and Justin, I am not Mother Theresa! I am still human, still a work in progress and still learning. I knew there would be setbacks, if I got angry or had more than I could handle I would just have to hit the release valve.

As a child my father was the most wonderful daddy to me. He was always kind, loving and patient with me. He was always very protective of me regarding my safety. I would say, quite over protective. He wouldn't let me do anything that might cause me harm. He was always gentle and kind. It was he who nurtured my love of nature and my awareness of the unseen world, whether he knew it or not. He was always spinning stories about the fairies and the natural world. As a child I never doubted any of his stories, they were facts to me. During my childhood, Mamma and Daddy would take walks with me in the woods by our house. It was something we did often. I always looked forward to these walks together and I remember them vividly. The woods were filled with beauty, mystery and awe. Whenever we would come across a fallen tree that had left a mound of dirt behind, Daddy would tell me that one of the Native

Americans was buried in that spot, giving me great respect for the woods. (It took me a while to figure out that wasn't true.) He would point out bird's nests for me to see, many with eggs for me to gaze upon. If the nest happened to be empty we would bring the nest home to our collection of other bird's nests. Once we were back at home he would point out the different materials that the bird had used to make its nest. I have always had a bird's nest collection and do at the present. Daddy built a case to place a collection of birds' nests he had gathered and gave it to me for my birthday not long ago. While in the woods we would look at the mosses and the lichen, admiring its beauty and color. It did not matter what time of year that we took our walks, there was always something beautiful to look at with awe. I am grateful to my father and mother for the wonderful walks we took, spending time together. These are very special memories that I have and cherish. I can still feel the love and tenderness that was present between us and it brings tears of joy to me as I remember.

However, as I grew into a young woman my father pulled back from me emotionally and physically. I could feel that he was uncomfortable being close with me. He no longer hugged me affectionately. He would barely put his arms around me. I was deeply saddened by this. It was the young children that he felt most comfortable around. It would remain that way for the rest of my life, although I still hugged him and kissed him, though not as I would have like to. I just had to remind myself that he loved me still, although it was not in the way I had wanted.

After I was older I could see and understand that his life had left some very deep emotional scars on him. As a child of less than four, he witnessed the death of his father. He said he remembered it vividly. He told me that he watched his daddy bend down to tie his shoe and then collapse onto the floor. His father died from an enlarged heart. The day his father died, thrust his entire family into the beginnings of a very deep poverty. His father had been a co-owner of a wood factory, but something very wrong happened. His mother was forced or left out of the business from that day forward. This was in 1925; women could not get loans and could hardly get jobs. It seems women did not matter much during those times. The power was out of balance and the masculine was in complete control. The four older children, including my father, were taken from their mother by the state and placed into an orphanage in Oxford, North Carolina for a time or until their mother could afford to take care of them. Daddy would tell me stories about the orphanage. They were sad and bitter stories. He said one of the lady orderlies was mean to him and he called her a bitch; she warned him if he said that word again she would put a bar of soap in his mouth. He did, he said it again. His father had raised dogs; "bitch" was a term he had heard often, none the less, he ended up with soap in his mouth. He told me part of their chores was picking up horse manure off the streets and keeping coal in the furnace room. He often talked about the work they had to do while in the orphanage. It was hard for me to hear and believe some of the things he told me. He was only four or five years old at that time. He said his oldest brother had run away from the orphanage to become a railroad bum, jumping on and off cars at his pleasure. Daddy said they would see him from time to time and nicknamed him Dusty, because of the dirt he always had on him. I am not sure how long they were sentenced to the orphanage, but it left its mark upon my father. His memories were very distressing. I heard him reference the orphanage many times in my life.

He, his brother, Howard and sister, Polly were allowed to leave the orphanage and return home after their mother had remarried. I think it was a couple of years before she married a gentleman much older than herself. He was kind to the kids and my father referred to him as, Pop. They would have two more children together. He ran a general store until the times got so bad that they were forced to close the store and find a place to live, any place. Daddy told me they were so poor, that they would find any old empty house and live there until they were forced to leave or were run off of the property. Daddy had gone to school on and off and finally quit in the sixth grade. At one time he was left alone in an old abandoned house with only his dog for companionship. His Mom and Pop went to see about a sick family member in a nearby city. He said that he and the dog ate crawfish and canned meat. I asked him if he was scared staying there in an old house by himself and he said, no not as long as his dog was there with him, he wasn't afraid.

When he was fifteen years of age he joined the Civilian Conservation Corp, the CCC's as he called it. It was an income where there had been none. He had lied about his age as I am sure that many young men did back then. He joined the Army at eighteen, fighting in World War II and the Korean War. He was discharged from the army several times but would rejoin because he couldn't find work, or he would be drafted again. He joined the service and was discharged 7 times in the course of twelve years.

He returned home often to visit his mother and step dad while on leave. He told me about being beside his step day on the day he died. He said that he saw his step dad's spirit leave his body after he passed away. I asked him; why do you think you saw your step dad's spirit leave his body? He never gave me an answer, but he knew what he had seen with his own two eyes. I thought he was allowed to see his stepdad's spirit leave his body as a reminder that there was more to life than what he had seen and experienced. It was a buoy for him, although seemingly small. It was sufficient to do the job. He carried that sight with him all his life and it profoundly affected his view of the afterlife, knowing there was more to life than meets the eye.

Although he didn't have an education, he was a smart man. He could do all kinds of work. He had many skills. I saw that from the things he had built, from the literature he read and the jobs he held. But I think from his point of view he felt self conscious and inferior to his peers. He had grown up in poverty and without an education. He was a small man. He said they all called him Baby Ray in the Army. His childhood and the wars left an emotional scar upon him that he could not seem to escape.

It was after my mother had passed and he was alone for those ten years that his drinking had gotten out of control and he would allow all of the awful memories of poverty from his childhood and sad and awful memories of the wars to take over. He had always told the family stories about the war, but after we moved back to live with him this time he talked about the war and his childhood almost every day. He would become upset and angry, very angry. He blamed the government and the wealthy. There was little or no aid for the poverty stricken when he was growing up. He resented how the wealthy lived very comfortable while he and his family had nothing, literally nothing. He remembers being looked down upon like he was trash. I asked him to let it go, I told him I did not mean that he had to forget it, but just let it go. He said he couldn't let it go.

He was a character, a delight in many ways, but he had a way of saying things that would just send anyone into biting their tongue, running away or putting up their fists. I was his usual victim of choice when it came to venting his anger. I would take his venting for as long as I could. It could go on for days and then I would have to let off my own steam. The next day would be like nothing ever happened between us. It was when he was drinking that it became unbearable for me to listen to his bitter words, although I knew that it was the alcohol, it still hurt to hear and to witness. He could turn on me in an instant and be angry in a second. The alcohol would just complicate the situation and bring out all of the emotion that he held in all his life.

What you saw is what you got with my mother and my father, but my father didn't sugar coat any of his words. If they every argued it would be over money. My father was who he was and he gave no pretense. I knew what I was getting into moving back. He was not going to change. With my father you knew he was not going to say what you wanted to hear just so you could hear it. He said what he was thinking. I think it was a big part of the spell he cast over people and the charm he exuded while saying it. For example, I was told by a friend of my father's about a time when they were in the grocery store line. There was a rather large lady in front of my father and he said something about, maybe the fat lady would let them in front of her, when she turned around to see who had said those words, my father flashed his big mega watt grin and she smiled and turned back around.

He was a good looking man and his gift to the world was his beautiful smile. He used that smile often. At ninety one he would flash his smile to any pretty girl that was nearby. He was not aware of it but, he had a charismatic charm about him. He would piss off our neighbor and friend Rick often. Daddy and Rick played poker, a game daddy loved, especially if he was winning and he usually did. Rick would get so angry with daddy sometimes that he would leave, vowing not to return, only to be back within a few days, apologizing to my father. My father could hold a grudge. He could also charm someone into doing, getting or giving him something he wanted. He had a way about him that I could not explain. I think his honesty of being himself, of being who he was, seemed refreshing in this day and time. He also had a sense of humor and would be picking much of the time.

Now that you have an idea of why I was a little reluctant to move back; you will understand why I would have felt a little better if I could have kicked and screamed. Even as sad as I felt, I still knew there were reasons for this move I did not yet understand. I had to have faith and know that there was more to our move back to Statesville than was on the surface. I had to be open and allow. I kept having thoughts about missing Justin and Casey, my family and my spiritual friends. Wilmington has many spiritually minded people. I was going to miss the strong ties that were formed. I knew I would also miss the spiritual gatherings and teachings. It would be up to me to continue learning, listening and allowing on my own.

For whatever reason, a very special revelation came before our move back to Statesville. I thought it was an invitation to come back to the farm, to be aware of what it had to offer. When the Universe wants you to receive something, whether it is knowledge or physical gifts, it does not matter who or how that knowledge or gift is presented. The Universe provides the way, the people and the situation. Remember, those miracles happen every day.

The Gifts

~≪⋙~

Several months before moving back to Statesville, we had gone home to visit my daddy. We hadn't been there long when my father laid out four crystals on the counter. My eyes got big and I asked him where he got the crystals. He told me they had come from the springs. He knew that I always had a special interest in stones. He and mama both liked all kinds of rocks, stones and crystals. He had bought a few tumbled stones for me when I was a young child. I was very excited to see these four crystals! I was also excited that he had found them in the springs at the pond on the farm. To me that made them even more special. He gave them to me for safe keeping, knowing that they would never leave my possession. As you will see from their descriptions and metaphysical properties, these four stones are very unique crystals. I consider them a special gift from the Universe, spirit.

The first crystal I am going to describe is the smallest and the most powerful stone of the four, being a very high vibration stone. It is called Clear Phenacite. It carries the properties of quartz as well as aids in interdimensional travel. It also facilitates accessing vibratory spiritual states that would not normally be reached from earth. It activates memories of earlier spiritual initiations and teaches that "like attracts like," urging you to raise your vibrations, purify your thoughts and put out positive energy. The spirit of this stone is profoundly joyful and teaches that life, and spiritual evolution should be fun. It is an extremely powerful activator for the crown and higher crown chakras. It produces a "fountain effect" in which golden energy pours in from the highest realms of being. It is a very clear quartz crystal about two inches long and one inch in height. It appears to have, what looks like, a city skyline on one side, like the dwellings that were carved into a mountain side. The other sides of the crystal are uneven, but smooth. It has several rainbows inside of it when held in the proper light.*

The second stone is a quartz crystal called Candle Quartz, another high vibration stone. It is so named because it looks like melting wax. Candle Quartz is said to be a light-bringer for the planet and those who have incarnated to help the earth change vibration. It also carries the generic properties of Quartz. Highlighting the soul purpose and focusing on the life path, it assists in putting ancient knowledge into practice. Candle Quartz is said to create tranquility and confidence. It is also helpful in understanding how the physical body is damaged by emotional or mental stress, and for healing the heart.*

The third crystal is Fenster Quartz. It has natural triangle formations within the planes of the crystal. These planes can be traversed as an inner landscape and stimulate clairvoyance. In addition to carrying the generic properties of Quartz, Fenster Quartz heals dysfunctional patterns and outgrown emotions and is excellent for sending healing light and for energy work that requires a high vibration. It can throw light on the past-life causes of addiction and remove them. It too, is a high vibration stone.*

The fourth stone is Black Tourmaline. This stone protects not only earth, but also protects against electromagnetic disturbance, radiation and negative energy of all kinds. It not only carries the generic properties of Tourmaline. Black Tourmaline is the most effective blocker of psychic attack and ill wishing. It instills a positive attitude no matter what the circumstance and stimulates altruism and practical creativity.*

It was a lot of fun to look up the metaphysical properties of these crystals and know the messages that each of these stones brings forth. I am most honored that these crystals found their way into my hands and my heart. It is a beautiful honor in deed to have had these four very unique stones to be found at the springs on the farm. I consider it a further confirmation of the work that I plan on doing here at the farm.

I was so intrigued by the crystals that after we moved back to the farm, I asked my father upon several occasions, where exactly had he had found the stones at the springs. I had gone to the springs multiple times, digging and digging; nothing, no other crystals did I find. I continued to ask him where he found the crystals and he said in the vegetable garden. I looked at him completely perplexed. He finally gave me an explanation after my third asking. I don't think he was intentionally not telling me how he found them; I think he had to remember how exactly, he did come across the crystals and how he came to find them in the vegetable garden. It seems that when he expanded the pond and had the walls of the spring enlarged, the soil that was dug out of the wall of the spring was taken up to the vegetable garden area. The soil was then spread out with the tractor and plowed under. That is how he came across the crystals. That was all I needed to know. I can only say, they were meant to be found! What a journey they have had. I have kept this knowledge and excitement very close to my heart.

Serenity Farm

Everyone who comes to visit us on the farm talks about how peaceful it is. They comment on the beauty of the land, about the rolling hills and emerald green grasses. It does offer a peaceful rest from the hustle and bustle of everyday life. I have always loved the land and had missed the openness it offered. I had always referred to our home place in Statesville as "The Farm". I began calling it Serenity Farm after our last return. Terry and I began preparing the farm to be a retreat, a place that people could come, rest, rejuvenate and heal. We planned for it to be open to anyone who would like to come and visit or come and stay for a couple of days. It is a quiet and tranquil place to rest, unwind and rejuvenate. There are many places for quiet reflection or meditation. The energy here is amazing!

With all the work we were doing, it took me a little time to be still long enough and really look at the farm. I had always loved it. I had missed the openness and tranquility it offered. I began taking walks to the springs and pond almost daily. There is always a serene beauty at the springs, combined with the sounds of nature that speak to my heart, offering quiet solitude and time for inner deliberation. On one particular walk to the springs, I became aware of the energy I was feeling. As I got closer to the springs a calming sensation came over me, I felt chills run up my back and I knew that I was in a vortex of spiritual energy. A vortex can be explained as an area that has a "thinning", all of the energies are present. This beautiful energy swept over me, taking me into a higher dimension of being. I knew in that moment that I was walking upon Sacred Ground. I could feel the energies lifting me into a higher vibration of energy.

As children we were always free to be out of doors here on the farm, to run and play and just have fun. Me, my nieces and nephews would go to the springs almost every time we were out of doors, it was like we were being called to the area. There was an old mulberry tree with a huge limb that jutted out from the trunk. The limb was not very far off the ground because the main trunk was on lower ground in the area of the springs. On that old limb was a perfect "saddle" that we children could mount easily and ride all day. We took turns riding in that saddle. The limb had just enough give and bounce that we could ride up and down, with our feet barely touching the ground. We could ride fast or slow. The old limb allowed us children to ride upon her for many years, until our legs grew too long to sit comfortably. We called her our Horsey Tree and rode on her every chance we got. Such fond memories it brings back for me to tell you about that wonderful tree. I am crying as I am writing these words. They are happy tears. There was so much fun and laughter at this very special place. Not only did we have fun, but this beautiful tree also gave us mulberries to eat. It has long been gone. She was quite an old tree old when I was a child.

To give you a mental picture of the springs, I will try to describe it as I see it in my mind's eye. There are five natural springs that feed the pond. The main spring comes up from the ground in a smooth trickle. At the top of the first spring is a high knoll with beautiful emerald green moss growing upon it. This area of the springs is filled with small underground tunnels; at one place is a mound of what looks like natural cobble stones. At the present time, we do not have cobble stones in this area. The stones look as if they have been carefully and intentionally placed by hand over the site. It was definitely a site of great personal attention for someone. It looks like a burial site. A smaller tree of maybe thirty some years of age is now growing out from the stones. As you continue south from the first spring, the other springs are dotted along the way, their water coming together with the first spring. Beautiful, huge Sugar Maples are growing by the water, reaching high into the sky. The area is dotted with dogwoods, ferns and holly trees. The area is shaded and cool in summer. Blue-gray clay is present within the banks of the spring. It is the kind of clay that is used to make pottery. The clay is smooth and firm, very pure in form without much secondary by-product.

The water coming up out of the spring is clean and clear. It appears to be a trickle, but its flow is constant. It was our source of drinking water when I was a child. We moved to the farm in the mid 60's. It was my older brother, Jerry's job to retrieve water from the springs each day. It was a difficult chore; the house is located some 600 feet west from the springs, at the top of the hill. It is a rather steep hill, that I often refer to as heart attack hill. The farm has a rolling terrain, with evergreen trees, deciduous trees and open pasture land. I recently had the ph of the water from the farm checked. It is a perfect 7.0.

The pond was built and is fed by the water from the springs. It was built almost fifty years ago and is home for much wildlife. Not only are there fish in the pond, but there are also turtles, snakes, deer, raccoons and many varieties of birds, geese, ducks, cranes, hawks, eagles and owls. We also have had foxes to raise their little ones at the springs. On the back side of the pond is a creek that runs east to west, while the springs run north to south. As you walk to the east from the pond you can stand at the edge of the pasture and look toward the south and down into the rather rapidly flowing creek. You can hear the water as it rushes by gushing over large rocks and boulders. It feels like looking down the side of a cliff when viewing the creek from the pasture. It is a very steep drop to the water.

We often walk down to the springs when family comes to visit. On this particular walk while at the springs, I felt we were not alone. I knew that spirits were close by. I felt chills coming up the right side of my back all the way up to my neck as we were stooped down looking into the water. I acknowledged them aloud and then they were gone.

I asked a friend, Reverend D. to come for a visit. She is and has been an intuitive since birth. An intuitive is one who can feel, sense, know, read timelines from the past and future, without the need for logic. She tells me that yes; there is a vortex at the area of the springs. She said that the Native Americans came to these springs to gather together. It was a sacred gathering place for many different tribes. In her mind's eye she could see the mothers putting a finger to their pursed lips, telling the children "shhhhhh", to be quiet. She said that ceremonies were held at the springs. All came, men, women, children and the elderly. She also said that some of the Native Americans had requested to be buried here or had died on the journey. Over the years my father has found many arrowheads and artifacts while plowing for his garden. We have not disturbed the soil in the area surrounding the springs. Who knows what we may find! I have recently come to know that there is a second body of water, not on our property but very close by. This would place my father's garden in the middle of two water sources; a good place to gather and have water nearby on either side.

When my mother and father bought this farm it was and had been a boot legers' property with only a small dirt road to get to the farm from the main road. The farm had deep red clay gullies running throughout the property. Many bottles of liquor and broken glass were found on the land and pieces of glass are still found today. My mother and father had a deep love for the land. Much grass seed, bull dozer work and sweat have been put into the farm by my parents. My mother and father built their house over the foundation of the original old home. The huge rocks that were used as foundation piers are still in place, although out of sight. I consider my mother and father as the care takers of this property. Terry and I could not be doing what we are doing without the effort and hard work they lovingly put into the farm and land. Terry and I are getting to put the frosting on the cake, with the finish work and beautification we are completing. I think of my parents' work as the restoration of the land; it can once again be recognized as the sacred ground, it has forever been and will always be.

We still have the flower gardens here at Serenity Farm that my mother started, almost fifty years ago. Some of the Peonies she brought with her to this farm are more than fifty years old. They continue to thrive and bloom year after year. I have since named the gardens, the Four Winds Garden, the Remembrance Garden, and the newest garden that Terry and I added, the Gated Garden. There is also an apple tree that was here when we moved to the farm. It drops the best old fashioned tart apples, making for a most delicious apple pie and fried apple pies. It is a large sized apple, being mostly green, with a blush of red. Terry and I want to take stem cuttings and grow the old fashioned apple tree onto graft stock. There are also many grape vines and arbors on the farm. Wild blackberries dot the landscape in summer. Persimmons will be ripe and on the ground sometime in late fall.

Before making our move back to the farm, I came to find out there were more gifts awaiting us. The second gift was a most wonderful surprise. Again, we had gone home to visit and check on my father before moving back. It was about a week or more before we were to make our final move back to the farm. We had just come in the house, settling in from the drive and talking with Daddy, when we heard a knock at the back door. It was Rebecca, our tenant who lived in the house on the hill, the house that Terry and I had built over thirty years ago on family land. I saw a look of dismay on Rebecca's face as she entered the house. It was obvious that she was tired, exhausted. She said she needed to ask me a favor and I said "OK". She told me that she and her family had been trying to load the horses for several hours that evening in preparation for the early morning departure they had planned. She said all the horses were loaded but two. She said that these two horses were not going to load. Rebecca and her family were preparing to move back to Texas. They had nine horses and had gotten all of the horses loaded with the exception of these two, a mare named Reno and her three month old foal, named Iris. Rebecca said that they had pulled and pushed on this mare for six hours on and off, trying to get her into the trailer. Reno had already kicked in the side of the trailer, broken the fence, broken a halter and cut her face. She was not going to load into the trailer. All were exhausted. Rebecca asked me if I would take these two horses. Would I take these two horses? Hmmmm, I did not hesitate to say yes, although it was going to be another ten days or so before we would be moving back.

My father had agreed to water and feed the horses until our return, but it seems he had other ideas about them, evidently. Within a day a two after returning home, we received a call from one of the neighbors saying that a man was in the pasture trying to catch the horses. I immediately called another neighbor and asked for her help. She went up to the empty house where the horses were. As she began talking with the man who was after the horses, she recognized him. She called him by name and said he was a horse trader. He had been at the houses to turn off the power and told my father he would buy the two horses from him. I don't know what my father was thinking, but I was so angry I could have spit nails. I had our neighbor to tell the man they were not my father's horses to sell. They belonged to someone else. That was the end of his pursuit. I then called Rebecca and asked her to please email me a bill of sale or proof of ownership for Reno and Iris.

These two horses had to be one of the happiest surprises of my life. I was very excited to have them on the farm with us. When I was around thirteen years old my father had won two horses playing poker. One of the horses was a mare; I named Ginger and her three year old filly that I named Sugar Baby. I knew nothing about horses, but I fell in love with Sugar Baby and I was the first person upon her back. She was a kind, gentle and affectionate horse. It turned out to be a very short, but intense relationship, especially for a thirteen year old girl. After school one day, I had come home to find both of them gone. My father had sold them without my knowledge. I have buried that day so deep into my subconscious that I do not remember my reaction. I imagine it was one of great sadness, anger and loss. My father told me after our return home this time, some forty years later, that Sugar Baby had died within a year of being sold. I asked him what had happened to her and he said "Heart Break". He knew we had a special relationship. I knew that my heart had been broken too.

For me to receive these two beautiful creatures from the Universe was a truly wonderful gift, although I had not had any horses since Sugar Baby, nor had I been around horses. It would be a learning curve. At the age of 54 I was going to educate myself about horses, learn about horses and eventually train horses.

As soon as we got a little settled from the move the first thing we had to do was we put up a fence around the pasture for them. They were in need of some shelter from the sun and the rain. We had a barn that would suffice that need for now. The weather was hot and humid, the flies and mosquitoes were hungry and the grasses were up to our knees. Most of the work fell on Terry's shoulders. He frantically worked getting the fencing around the pasture. He suffered from bug bites, poison ivy and heat. We wore a wet cloth around our neck to keep us cooler and still I could not take the heat like he could. I am sorry to say I was not much help for him. When he had finished the fence we waited for the whole Wilmington family to come that weekend so that we could witness the horses make their virgin trip into the big pasture. It was a beautiful site. We opened the fence so they could enter into the "new" pasture. The horses were excited to see and eat that tall and luscious grass. They walked slowly into the new pasture, checking out the unfamiliar ground before going into a full gallop, kicking, bucking and (farting) along the way. It brought joy to all of us to witness such an event. The horses were so obviously happy.

I didn't think that Reno was a very friendly horse, but then I understood what was going on. I was told she had been picked at by the kids. They threw sticks at her and poked at her, teased her. My trust would have to be earned. She did allow us to touch and work with her baby foal, Iris. As I got to know them a little better, I added a second name to both of the horses, Lady Reno and Iris Athena. After our move these two horses were always the highlight of my day. I could go outside and be with them, grooming them from the fence, watching them, observing them, any cares I may have had would disappear from my thoughts. I told my sister-n-law, Jean the only thing they were missing were wings and I really believe they have them too, I'm just not seeing them.

The first summer we had the two horses I was afraid of Reno, she would pen her hers back over the slightest move from us. Terry would be inside the fence grooming her and I could tell she liked and enjoyed it, most of the time. She would breathe a sigh of relaxation and bend her leg, resting one of her hips; her mouth would be open enough for her lower lip to be relaxed and slightly quivering. I watched Terry with jealously. I wanted to be in the corral grooming her, not just reaching over the fence and grooming her from time to time. I had to get over my fear of Reno.

I had to make some changes. I had to summon the courage to go in the corral and groom Reno and so I did. The first day I went in with her everything was going well. I was bent over combing her leg when I heard her mouth open. I was startled and stood up immediately; she was just getting something out of her mouth. I had to laugh at myself. I started educating myself about horses, their behaviors, how to work with them and train them effectively without any aggression on my part. I quickly found out I had to be the Alpha horse. I had to be the leader, someone they could trust to protect them.

In the mean time we bought two more horses, both needed rescuing, one was way too skinny and the other, was emotionally hurt. I was quickly developing quite the affinity for horses. I bought books on horses. I read about horses online and then I found the person I really wanted to immolate, Pat Parelli. He has a way with the horses that is absolutely beautiful. He respects and understands the horse's nature. His training is centered on partnering with the horse, while gaining the trust of the horse. He is aware of the difference in horse personalities and how to work with each personality to bring about the easiest learning scenario. I bought his training DVD's and began to educate myself on his training of horses. Through my learning about horses, I made up my mind and got the courage to enter the corral with them. We now have a round pen where we work individually with each horse. The Parelli' methods of horse training were both respectful to the horse and the horse's nature and presented a safe approach to the training for both horse and person. I then began to read about various herbs for the horses. I wanted to assist and nurture the horse as naturally as I could. Although sometimes our man made medicines have been required. I read about how the pasture is the horses pharmacy, with different herbs (most all of us call them weeds) that the horse will eat as needed. I have even befriended an Equine Herbalist from Ireland on Facebook. If there is a natural way to approach the horse in all matters, that is what I will choose.

Many people want horses and have horses but they forget that they are horses. They are boarded and shut up all the time. This does not make for a healthy or happy horse. It is going against their natural way of being. Some people forget that the horse is a herd animal and needs companions. Most people forget that the horse likes to put its head down and eat grass. I have come to decide that the needs of the horse, (my horses) come first when it is at all possible. We now have eight horses on various pastures on the farm. Most of them are rescue horses, from either emotional or physical harm. It gives me and Terry great satisfaction to interact with the horses, to see them in such great condition. The horses teach me something every day. We do little riding on the horses for now, but I am sure that will come.

According to Dr. Robert Miller in his book, "Understanding the Ancient Secrets of the Horse's Mind", he compares the horse to the donkey. He states that neither the donkey nor the horse forgets anything; the donkey is considered stubborn, the horse is not. Dr. Miller states the donkey does not forgive whereas the horse is very forgiving.

Dr. Miller also talks about the horse as a precocial species, which means it, is neurologically mature at birth. He says that it is common for the newborn of prey species. To give you an example, newly hatched chicks, ducklings, goslings, quail, grouse, newborn fawns, calves, lams and foals are fully active soon after birth. Unlike kittens, bear cubs, puppies or newly hatched owls or hawks, all of which are predatory species and are born quite helpless at birth. The precocial species must be quickly able to recognize danger and flee from it.

The horses are a big part of Serenity Farm Retreat. Horses teach us humans many things. They assist in healing from a spiritual standpoint as well as physical and emotional. They are truly a gift to us humans. It is my intent that persons with chronic or terminal illness, the physically or emotionally challenged will come and experience healing empowerment through horses, farm animals and nature. Horses help people to process their emotions, bringing happiness. I consider myself an ambassador for the horse. To see through the eyes of a horse is beyond words. You must be a leader and be trust worthy before the horse will consider you as such.

A Little Perspective

Let me teach you.

When you are tense, let me teach you to relax.
When you are short tempered, let me teach you to be patient.
When you are short sighted, let me teach you to see.
When you are quick to react, let me teach you to be thoughtful.
When you are angry, let me teach you to be serene.
When you feel superior, let me teach you to be respectful.
When you are self absorbed, let me teach you to think of greater
    things.
When you are arrogant, let me teach you humility.
When you are lonely, let me be your companion.
When you are tired, let me carry the load.
When you need to learn, let me teach you. After all, I'm your horse.

W. Lamm
1997

The Horses of Serenity Farm

I want to give you a brief description of our horse friends here on the farm. They are each beautiful, unique and wonderful teachers of life.

Lady Reno, our first horse at Serenity Farm. She is a beautiful flea bitten grey quarter horse. She has thousands of little red dots in her hair. She has big beautiful dark eyes that pierce through your heart. She talks to you in low tones with her lips barely moving as she awaits her morning feed or any treat she may receive. She is most affectionate when you are close, without eye contact. She will come in close to investigate and smell. She gently lifts her head to avoid ever hitting you when she is close. She teaches me trust in her and trust in myself. She is a very big horse. Did I mention she is pigeon toed?

Iris Athena is Lady Reno's three year old filly. She is a big beautiful deep roan colored quarter horse, with a white blaze on her face in the shape of the number one. She is self assured in all ways, teaching me to take pride in myself. I call her our Ambassador Horse, the diplomat, teaching us about "political grace". She can get along with all of the horses when she chooses to do so. It is she who comes to welcome all new visitors, horse, person, dog or cat. She is very graceful and muscular. She will often hold water in her mouth after drinking, until you extend your hand to rub her and then she opens her mouth to let the water spill on you. She reminds me a little kindness goes a long way. She teaches me life is fun.

Next, on the list is our Chico Amigo. He is a very tall Tennessee walking horse, with big, kind, eyes. He is a beautiful, dark chocolate color, almost black that glistens in the sun. Chico has two white socks on the back feet. He is amazingly beautiful with enough mane and tail for several horses. He teaches me patience and grace as he leads the herd. He has a calm endurance, being very tolerant, especially with Iris who is always, nipping, picking, rearing up and playing with him. He teaches me composure and self assurance.

Cheyenne Jewell is our liver chestnut and white, tobiano paint. She teaches me that I have to have the right motivational choices to get her moving. She is always motivated by a treat. Once a bit stand offish, she now comes for the occasional scratch or grooming. She teaches me acceptance and caring as she trains and grooms her foal.

Casey's Lakota or Little Bit, as I have nick named her is Cheyenne's foal. She is a beautiful little overo paint filly with a thick white mane and tail that has a little dark hair blended in. She has big dark eyes that peek out from the white of her mane. Little Bit has a lot of moxey. She is one of the youngest horses in the herd, but she will stand up for herself if need be. She won't be pushed around unnecessarily. She teaches me to use discernment.

Seminole Sami is our black and white paint gelding. I call him Sami, sweet boy horse. He is gentle and shy, one of the last in the pecking order. He teaches me it is okay not to be first. He also teaches us about being sensitive. He teaches us to pay attention.

Snow Jewell is a beautiful Arabian Cross mare, a flea bitten grey that we rescued. She had a bacteria/fungus called rain rot that was so severe that we had to call the vet out. She was about 150 pounds under weight when we got her and she had a young colt that was nursing. This condition is contagious and she and her colt had to be quarantined in a separate pasture. It took about three months to get her back to health and for her to regain some of her lost weight safely. She is one of the kindest and sweetest horses I have ever been around. She has taught me steadfastness and loyalty with her always optimistic attitude. Life is joyful.

Pepper Jack is Snow Jewell's colt. His sire was a black quarter horse but he has taken back after his Arabian Cross dame. He is small and quick. He was born almost pure black. He has the gray gene and will gray out over the years. Right now he looks like a buck skin. He still has very black legs. He was untamed when we got him. On our first meeting in the pasture, he raised up on his hind legs. I laughed and told him we would have none of that. We could not touch him. He was jumpy, skittish, always biting us. We had to separate him from his mother to wean him and have him gelded. Sami was his companion horse and baby sitter. They remain very close. Pepper is our little miracle horse. We thought we would never get him tamed and trained. He is a star student. He halters, leads and backs up. He doesn't mind being touched anywhere and has started whinnying a hello in the mornings as his dame does. He teaches me to reserve my judgment, to be patient and allow. All good things come in time.

Renovating the Old Barn

In 2012, during and in the middle of rescuing horses, we needed to do some major repairs to the old barn. Its' age is unknown, but it like the old house sits on huge rocks for the foundation piers. The main seal for the support of the barn was failing in several places and we needed to shore it up and make it more secure. We also planned to remove an old, rotten and dilapidated cow shed that was attached to the barn and build a new shed with four stalls, suitable for the horses. The old shed was completely full of junk and discarded material, as well as being unsafe and ready to fall down. We planned on tearing off the old tin roof. It was only being held to the barn and shed by a few rusty nails and was ready to fly away with the next hard wind.

We began by emptying the barn. It had grown into a glorified storage shed, with more recyclable material (junk) than anyone needed. You have to remember; my father was raised during the depression and experienced the depression first hand. It left its' mark on many. My father throws nothing out if there is a slight chance that it could be used later. He was recycling long before it became fashionable. It was always out of necessity in his mind. At the time we were going to begin our barn project, Daddy was recovering from hernia surgery and could not get out and around as much as he liked to. It was probably better for all of us, as we had to throw out a lot of recyclable material. I tried to be respectful of the things he really told us he wanted to keep. It took several trips to the local county trash and recycling center to get it all hauled off. It was a job just getting the barn emptied and hauled off.

We could now begin the task we had before us. Terry bought two four ton house jacks. He planned on using the jacks to lift the barn a section at a time. We began with the southeast corner of the barn. I was a little nervous about the lifting, you could hear the wood creek and crack and make noises while he was lifting the weight of the barn from the seal. He had two helpers on this part of the project. It was something he could not do by himself or with me alone. Some of the seals had to be cut out, removed and replaced completely, some partially. As we got further along into the repairs we could see that the termites had done a lot of damage, more than we ever suspected. Terry started tearing down the old barn siding that had termite damage. It was very apparent that we needed to replace most of the siding.

We have a friend and neighbor with a saw mill less than two miles down the road. We used cut to order planks which helped to save lots of money on the lumber. We would place small orders of wood as it was needed. We choose rough sawn pine for the exterior, giving the barn a very rustic look. We will have to paint or stain it sometime in the near future to keep it from rotting. After nine months of hard, hot and nasty work, we had a brand new looking barn. Although we had not planned to build a new barn, it has a lot of new wood in the repair work. We wanted to keep as much of the old barn that we could. It is a nice blend of the old with the new. The barn is very unique, functional and very attractive. Daddy was very proud of his new barn.

During the renovation of the barn I had taken many photos, before and after shots. Sometime during the renovation the family had come in for a visit and they were looking at some of the photos I had developed and had laying out for them to look through. Before heading back to Wilmington my nephew Jeremy was looking at the photos when he pointed out what looked like a huge light orb in one of the photos. I was very surprised, I had not seen it in the photos. I asked Terry, how did I miss that? After everyone left I got my reading glasses and magnifying glass to take a really good look at this photo again, what I saw absolutely delighted me. It was not a light orb, I had captured the spirit of a horse with its head out of the old barn window and I know who this horse is. Sugar Baby never really left. It is her sweet and kind spirit that gives the barn the wonderful energy that is felt.

The barn is a beautiful collection of things. It represents the old, the new and the spiritual. It has a very peaceful feeling to it as well. We used a left over chandelier to light the loft. It was supposed to be a temporary solution, but we like it so much that it will be a permanent fixture. We have two beautiful lights coming into the barn. There is a setting area with chairs and a table. A most wonderful sounding wind chime hangs in the middle of the breezeway as you enter the barn area.

The Passing of My Father

We have been at the farm for almost three years. I would have to say that I am at the best place that I have been at on my spiritual journey. I have made and found peace with myself and know this is where I am supposed to be at this time of my life. As I had just barely gotten started writing to you about the story of my sacred journey my father passed from this earth. I want to tell you about it in more detail.

It was in December of 2012 that I had gotten up out of bed to go to the bathroom in the middle of the night. For some reason I became very aware that he, my father would not be with us much longer. I knew he was getting up in years but this feeling was one I could not ignore. I was meant to know this, to know that he would pass very soon. I related the information I had gotten to my husband. My Father was in very good health for his age. He was already talking about the vegetable garden and growing his delicious tomatoes for the summer. We often talked about him living to be 100 years of age.

He never talked about dying as something he feared. He knew that when it was his time, it was his time. He was very matter of fact about his own passing. He had been through two wars as I had mentioned earlier and he had come out of both without a scratch. He said the only thing that happened to him was that he had to have hemorrhoid surgery. He told us that when they began the operation that the sedation didn't work and that he could feel the whole thing, he swore it to be so. We would always laugh as he went on and on about it. He told us about "missing in action" while on a ship. Again, we laughed. He said he had to go to the Brigg over it. He was always telling us war stories. Below is a photo of my daddy while he was in the Army. In another Army photo of daddy, as a little girl I asked him what he was looking at because all the other people were facing forward and he was looking to his left. He told me he was looking at the hoochy-goochy girls. I asked, "What are hoochy-goochy girls?" He tells me they are pretty girls.

I had always wanted for him to pass quickly on his tractor, or doing something that he enjoyed doing. I knew that he would not allow us to care for him. He would have been like one of the horses with a broken leg that has to be put down.

It was Casey's passing that he could not understand. He was sure that someone had given him something that killed him without him knowing about it. He thought that maybe someone had put pills into his candy. I tried to explain to him that Casey had taken a pill that he thought would make him feel better, ease his mental anguish, just like my father did with his alcohol. No matter how I tried to explain, he was not going to hear it or understand it. He could not believe that Casey had passed before him.

He spoke often about Casey sending the UFO ship for him. He said he was ready. One night I heard him muttering and kind of whimpering with fear, in his sleep. The next morning I told him about what I had heard and he said he had had a nightmare. He said there were people around his bed, short people. I asked, like me? He said, no, like little people. I asked, what did they look like and he said he couldn't tell because they had on hoods, that was why he was scared; he couldn't see their faces. I said you are always asking the extraterrestrials to come for you and when they did, you screamed out in fear. He laughed.

We got the local paper for my Father to read every day. He liked to read and to keep up with current matters. He told me about the kindergartners getting computers and I mentioned maybe he needed to learn about the computer. This is his reply. He said he didn't think so. He told me that he thought that he was learning about being a spirit. He said he was going to go where he wanted to, when he wanted to. That he would not have to eat and that Washington better watch out for hurricane Bob. We busted out laughing and he did too.

He didn't mind getting old. He said he didn't even know he was old until he looked in the mirror. The knowledge of seeing his stepdad's spirit leave his body had remained with him his entire life. I think that little buoy saved him much agony and grief over his own passing. It definitely colored his view of life after death. He knew there was more!

He referred to me as a white witch since my return home. In his mind a white witch is someone who does good and assists in healing. He often asked if I was doing brainwashing. I assured him

I was not interested in brainwashing. He was perfectly fine with me seeing and working with people who came to get energy healing, but he would not get on the table himself. It really didn't matter though. He liked me to take the pendulum and check the energy in his hands. It was always strong and going clockwise.

Within the past year, Terry had gone to the Veterans Administration and had gotten my father's VA benefits started. He got an extra $176 per month for time served. We decided to surprise him and get his medals reinstated, but they told us it would take several years for them to come in. Terry received a call from Brad at the Veterans office telling him the medals had come in. It was less than a year. Brad told Terry, he didn't know what we did, or who we called, but he had never seen medals arrive so quickly. I told Terry it was a sign and the end was nearing closer. We called the family and plans were made to surprise Daddy with a party and present him with his newly reinstated medals for Easter weekend. Thursday a week before Easter, he had been drinking pretty heavily. Terry and Rick, our neighbor, was going to help him to bed. I had gone out to feed the horses their evening hay. I was only gone for ten minutes, when I got back I knew that something had happened. Daddy was lying on his bed and Terry was holding a cloth to Daddy's head. While I was out it seems that Daddy had gotten up out of the bed and had gone past Terry and Rick tripping and falling head first, into the wall. His head hit the wall so hard that it cracked the sheetrock. He had hit the corner of a 2X4 stud in the wall, putting a four inch gash in his forehead. He needed stitches. He was so intoxicated that he would not allow us to help him. I was afraid to try and drive him to the hospital. We dialed 911. The paramedics arrived shortly and began assessing the situation. It took a little time, but they finally got him into the ambulance. We followed shortly behind in the car. Once at the hospital we learned that he had pulled the intravenous needle out of his arm. He was very agitated. They had to use restraints on his arms to be able to take the x-rays that were needed. He told me to get my pocket knife and cut of those—damn restraints. I explained they had taken my pocket knife at the entrance. We were at the hospital all evening, returning home late. My father was so sedated when we got home that Terry and I had to use an office chair to wheel him into the house from the car and get him to bed. He fell out of his bed that night; I had to call for Terry to help me to get him back into his bed. The next day he was throwing up all day long. Daddy told me he would have to slow down his drinking a bit to get over this and we agreed. When I called the hospital emergency room again, they wanted us to bring him back to the hospital so they could be sure that nothing had been missed on the MRI. Again, he was given the green light to go home. He was given medication to take home for the nausea. That evening I was on what I call, high alert during the night, listening in case I might be needed. I heard him talking in his sleep. He said, "Hi guys". His voice sounded happy and filled with surprise to see whoever it was. Then he said some Army slang, it sounded like ten hut. Later I heard him moving about in his room. I went in to check on him, he was getting dressed and ready. Each time I went in to check on him he was getting ready to get up, I would tell him what time it was and he would say, you want me to go back to bed, don't you? He stayed in bed until 3am before finally getting up out of his bed. He had an upset stomach the rest of the morning. When we got up that morning he asked me to look at his tongue. He thought it was swollen. As I looked I could sense that something was truly wrong. I thought that his death was very, very, close. I tried to call Justin, but to no avail. I went out to the barn to call my sister-in-law, Jean and told her that Daddy was not doing well. I told her the family might be coming for a memorial service instead of a surprise party to present his war medals, either way I knew that it was all as it should have been. All the family would be here.

As I went back into the house daddy was sitting at the kitchen counter. I called our neighbor Rick and told him he might want to come and see daddy this morning, knowing that daddy could take his leave shortly. Rick was at the house within a few minutes. I could tell that Daddy really didn't feel good at all. Rick asked Daddy if he would like to play poker and a big smile came over his face. Rick said that he was going to the grocery store and would be back within the hour. Terry was in his office at the computer working so I decided to take a quick shower. After getting dressed, as I came down the hall into the kitchen I heard Terry telling Daddy to let go of the chair and he would help him to his chair. He said, "Bob you've got to let go of this chair so I can get you to your chair." Just as I entered the room I could see daddy shaking and trembling all over and he collapsed onto the floor. I hurried into the room to get in back of Daddy as Terry was lowering him easily onto the floor. We each had him in our arms; his eyes were open and fixed, looking up and to the right. He was not breathing. There was neither in breaths, nor out breaths. Terry gently placed a pillow under his head him and then dialed 911 as I held Daddy in my arms talking to him and reassuring him that he was not alone and that the angels were all around him. I was so very thankful that I got to hold him in my arms, one last time. The paramedics arrived very shortly, working on him for twenty minutes or more until I asked the EMS team how long were they going to keep pushing, pulling and sticking needles into my father. I found their work to be disturbing, almost disrespectful, to my father at this point, but I also knew that they had a job to do.

I felt like my father had taken his leave in a very quick fashion. It was a good way to pass. I thought he was not scared, nor was he in any obvious pan. I thought it was a beautiful way to depart the physical. The EMS supervisor responded to my question and said they would stop after the last round, but then someone thought they saw eye movement and another thought they might have a pulse.

Off they went into the ambulance. After arriving at the hospital it would be another hour or so before Terry and I were allowed to see him. When I went into the emergency suite he was hooked up to all sorts of machines doing his body's work. He had a breathing tube down his throat. I barely recognized him. Tubes and needles were everywhere in his frail body. I sent him a kiss and then I told him to fly out of there! I did not want to see him like that. We left the room and were going to get some lunch, before we had even ordered any food I got the call saying that he had passed. In my heart he had passed at home, with his loved ones by his side.

Even though I had been aware that his passing was coming soon, it was still a bit of a shock. His passing had happened quickly and suddenly, but it had happened in a good way. I was happy, relieved, for him in that matter. I came home from the hospital to feel the sadness of allowing him to pass and knowing that he would not be here with us. His long sleeve garden shirt still hangs in the tomato shed where he had left it from last season. His straw hat sets on the work bench in his granary. Most all of his tools lay where he left them. I cried that evening knowing I would miss him not being here and it was something, as he would say, "Would take some getting used to". He was and will always be such a big part of this farm.

Everyone was sad that he didn't get to see his medals or that we didn't get to present them to him, but I knew he saw them and that he knew the whole story. He knows that the family wanted to do this out of our love and honor for him. The evening after his passing, as I shut my eyes for sleep that night, I kept seeing what looked like a search light in my vision. At first it was an invading light within my shut eyes. It swept by two times in my vision and then I realized, I knew, it was Daddy. It was his way of letting me know he was home and he was fine. I saw it for two nights in a row and I have not seen it since. I feel his presence here on the farm much of the time. Again, I know this is not the end, I will see him again. He is forever in my heart. He is surely missed and loved.

My father is the most recent of my family to make his translation into the non physical; it was unmistakably the easiest for me to accept for one reason. I know in my heart that the soul is eternal. This does not mean that I did not have feelings that I had to deal with, but there was much acceptance and happiness in my heart for my father's passing. Although I do not have all the answers or know all the questions to ask; I am content to know in my heart that he is fine. He will now know and remember all. All of the "good" and the 'bad' in this life and all the other lives he has led. He will know of his worth. He will know in his being that he is truly part of The All That Is. He will know of his divinity and heritage. He will be free. He will be loved and loving and he will just be. How can I not be happy for his soul? Any sadness I may feel is for myself and how I will miss my father not being on this earth with me. To explain this further, we think we feel sadness and grief when someone passes, but what we are really missing is how we felt in their presence. My heart knows that he will come again and again, in and out of life. It was not just accepting the fact that he was up in years (ninety-one) and had led a full life; although I am sure it played a part in my acceptance. This life is just a multi-second when compared to eternity. The knowledge I carry in my heart is what allows me to see and know, to have faith of life beyond this physical embodiment. With my father's passing, the Bridges' name will die out in our lineage. He was the last living male in his family; the other brothers either had no children or girls. I relayed this sadness to my cousin in California. She has kept her Bridges name. She said that before his passing that our Uncle Frank had allowed her to swab the inside of his cheek. She then sent his DNA sample to a genealogy lab. The lab indicated that he did carry the Bridges gene, but that, we as Bridges, are also related to many others as indicated by the genes. We have Viking and Native American genes in our DNA.

Since my Daddy's passing in early spring we have received what I call, many "gifts" from him. It warms my heart and puts a smile on my face to tell you about them. This year, Terry and I decided to wait and plant an early fall garden this season. It would be the first time in fifty years that a spring garden had not been planted here on the farm. We had many, many tomato plants to "volunteer" in the old unused chicken lot. Terry was able to transplant several plants into the garden area. As we walked and looked at the garden, we saw there were "volunteer" potatoes coming up in bunches. There is also a very stately sunflower that "volunteered"; it has a big beautiful bloom that is flourishing. Terry dug up the onions that my father had planted last fall. They are sweet and delicious. We thanked Daddy for his beautiful gifts and got the message loud and clear. We could hear him in our heart say something like this, "If you don't want to plant a garden this spring, at least eat these fresh potatoes, tomatoes and onions, oh, and enjoy the sunflower." He loved sunflowers!

As we make our journeys in and out of life we come as personalities that may or may not be recognized. We come in different sexes, and shapes. We take on the many different traits of the family we are in. There are so many different combinations, the choices are endless. The babies we love and hold in our arms may be our great, great, grandmother, our grandfather, or our sister or brother. We hold our babies as if they are new to this world, but in your arms may be one you have loved before. We are all family! What matters is, that it really does not matter, for true love is love. No matter what name we may call the ones we love we now have the chance to recognize the fact that the babies we hold have been here before, just as we have. We can make a difference in their lives, if we but see them as the soul and nurture their remembering. Allow them to speak openly from their heart as they remember, knowing that they are God in form. See their inner light and honor it. Let them know of their greatness! Let them know that they are the soul, a beautiful light created in the image of our Mother/Father. Empower them! "A human being is part of the whole called by us . . . "Universe" . . . a part limited in time and space. He experiences his thoughts and feelings as separate from the rest—a kind of optical delusion of his own consciousness. This delusion is a prison for us, restricting us to our own personal desires and to affection to a few persons nearest to us. Our task must be to free ourselves from this prison by widening our compassion to embrace all living creatures and the whole of nature and its' beauty . . ." Albert Einstein. I find the beauty of his mind to be of tremendous insight and support.

Walking the Sacred Path

The only thing that really ever changed about Casey's passing was my perspective on death, on life and on spirit. It was with this change in perspective that I am able to find happiness and joy in life again. I have shared my story with you in an effort to give you an opportunity to view our existence from another point of view. It is our choice as to whether we wish to remain asleep and live our life as the personality or recognize ourselves as the soul and live life fully incorporating our personality self with the soul. When we know that we are the soul twenty four hours a day, seven days a week and through eternity, we can live life more fully. We can appreciate all things. We can call on the resources of the Universe for assistance. We are truly one big family. This little earth and our lives are just a part of what is going on. This is just one of the realities that we are tapping into. We have many more abilities that are ours for the asking. We can tap into the super consciousness that is readily available for all, if that is what we wish. Please keep an open mind. Many people think they have an open mind when it is shut so tight the light of day cannot enter.

I pose the following questions to all of us. How can we continue to have wars and disputes over one's religious beliefs? How asinine is that? How can we have wars because someone has a different belief from our own? How can we continue to kill our brothers and sisters? How can we continue to dishonor our Mother Earth? She is alive. She is a living breathing, sentient being, having a consciousness. She loves us without conditions as a loving mother does and how do we respect her? Life is all around us, know this. We must learn to share this world if we are to survive and thrive.

Our family losing everything was not about finances at all, nor was it punishment, nor was it about learning about budgeting. It was a marker for me; it was about me stopping long enough to want to know more about life. It was the brake I placed in this life to assist me and prepare me for the next step of my life; to remember I am the soul.

To be happy and to have joy in our lives is one of our Creator's greatest gifts, but we must take the wheel and do the driving. We are responsible for ourselves and our personal happiness, no one else is. When we allow ourselves to be happy we feel beautiful from the inside out. It does not matter how handsome or pretty we think we appear from the outside. Happiness comes in all sizes, shapes, ages, colors and sexes. I would imagine that happiness is one of the most coveted of emotions. To some, happiness may seem so far away that it feels impossible to attain. I want to assure you that happiness is just around the corner and it is something that we all can have in our lives. You can have happiness and joy in your life. I am going to ask you to keep an open mind, believe in yourself and take part in the steps and actions that we are going to be aware of and learn. I know that I will be seeing a smile on your face and a glow in your aura very soon! I am setting my intent that my story and these words will fill all those who read it with LOVE eternal, knowing all things are possible.

If you have read my story you already know that happiness and joy are a part of our birthright. If you have a DESIRE that happiness and joy be a part of your life I am here to help you make that desire grow, to hold your hand as we go through a very positive and personal transformation. I will be addressing the whole person; mind, body and spirit. Before we begin our journey I want you to know that YOU are much loved. I want you to know of your worth. I want you to know of the power that you have to change your life. It does not matter what you have done, what you have thought, what you have said, in this life or any of your other lives. Every second is a new beginning. Miracles happen every day! So, quit making excuses. Take responsibility and find your joy. You deserve it! Remember you are more than this body. This life is a beautiful gift to enjoy. There is much love for you in the unseen world. Together, we are going to take steps to assist you in realizing just how valuable you are. Remember those precious little children you may love, you are one of those precious ones, just older. That inner child is still a apart of you. You are going to learn ways to love yourself, respect yourself and take care of yourself, from an emotional point of view. Please don't turn and run when I tell you that you are going to learn to take responsibility for yourself, your actions and your thoughts. You are probably wondering; what do thoughts have to do with being happy? I must tell you that your thoughts have everything to do with your happiness. Happiness is a state of being, it is not a destination. I am not saying you will be happy every moment of every day because life happens, but I am telling you that you will have the power to overcome obstacles in your life and see them for what they are, opportunities for growth and expansion. You will come to realize that you and only you have any power over you. You will know that you control the boat and you can stop paddling up stream against the current and just float along enjoying the scenery. Once found, happiness and joy only grow as you continue to expand your openness to allow. When joy is a part of your life, your heart is open and you are free to love not only yourself, but all of life.

I want you to be aware of the need to surround yourself with people who lift you up, not those who may try to control you or put you down. The only person or thing that we need to control is ourselves. We cannot control others and do not let others control you. Just say "no". We may try, unknowingly, to control others from time to time by use of guilt or manipulation, but really it is a waste of time that we could be using in a more productive way. You will start to notice manipulation instinctively whenever it is put in your path and you will be able to avoid it completely. Just say no. We do not want to manipulate others and we do not want to be manipulated. When we can look at our lives and find gratification from within we will find happiness and joy. It is not going to be found trying to make someone do something we want them to do, or say something we want them to say. Acting in a certain way will not bring us happiness. We all know that money does not buy happiness. It may make us happy for the short term, but for true happiness, we are going on a journey within. Look at the people in Hollywood who have all the money anyone could want and still many are not happy, have addictions, stress and depression. We will not find happiness trying or pretending to be something that we are not just to please or impress another. It is imperative that we learn to respect and honor all life, beginning with ourselves. If we do not honor and love self, how can we share something we do not have? Happiness is not found by manipulating or being manipulated using tactics of fear, or control, or anger. We are each here on this earth to learn and experience. We are here to be sovereign unto ourselves, being responsible to and for ourselves and for our actions. We can no longer blame others for the actions we take. Happiness and joy starts within and when one can recognize and know that they have the power to make this happen, life is never the same. That person can be you. When you are happy and joyful, it shows outwardly as well as within, you feel it and it is contagious. Happiness and joy are feelings that allow us to expand, to be comfortable in our own skin, to know that we belong on this earth; that we have a purpose for being here. Your light is contagious. We are able to know we are a part of the ALL. When we are living on purpose, happiness and joy come effortlessly. Happiness and joy allow our heart to sing. Your friends will want to know what you have just done. Your change will be obvious and noticeable. Your family, friends and co-workers will want to know what you have done. They will want to know why you are so happy. When you learn that you can be happy, it only grows as you allow yourself to enjoy the smallest of life's little pleasures. You will begin to savor all of the little joys life has to offer and you will begin to look at life through different lenses. You will be seeing life through rose colored glasses.

I know most of us have seen happy people and have wondered and asked these same questions. It seems some people are born this way. They hum and sing to themselves for no reason. I have a family member who used to hum as she ate. The food tasted so good to her and it made her happy, so she hummed as a result of being happy. I have known a little one who used to hum as he sat on the toilet. I know these examples sound a little strange but; these people have happiness/joy in their lives. Happiness is a state of mind. They just seem to be happy. You can have that happiness too. You deserve to be happy. It is a birthright. We are going to take the necessary steps to reclaim your personal happiness. You can share your empowerment with your family and friends, if you like. It is time now to set your intent to be happy and to find pleasure and joy in life every chance you get. Right now, I want you to look up, take a deep breath, let it out, and whether you say this silently or out loud, repeat these words: "It is my intent to be happy". I am not saying you are going to be happy twenty four hours a day. And yes, you are going to have to get involved and do a little work on yourself. The results will be tenfold.

The Body

We want to always take care of our body. This may sound trivial, but the body is the vessel that allows us to interact in our world. So we have got to have our body's needs taken care of. I would even say that we need to talk to our body and thank it for all that it does. Show your gratitude. Appreciate your body.

I am not suggesting that we need to be athletes, but if you are sitting on the sofa, huffing and puffing on cigarettes, watching TV all day, eating junk food, what are the chances you are going to feel good? The body is the vessel that we use here on Earth. Be grateful for such an amazing, wonderful and magnificent vessel to use. We need to take care of our body's needs. The basics of food, water, sleep, and exercise should always be taken into consideration. We want to have balance in all areas of our life. When we are tired or sleepy, or hungry we are not in our best disposition. We tend to get agitated, irritated and angry. We want to alleviate any of the negative tendencies that we can. Start by being aware and agreeing to take good care of your body. Remember, balance.

Letting Go

As I had mentioned earlier joy, happiness is a birthright. Many of us have had life circumstances in which all joy and happiness seems to have been taken, stolen from us, but we can let those feelings go. We do not have to remain the victim. Whether it is self imposed feelings of guilt or anger, or those feelings are aimed at others, the first step is to let it go, quit punishing yourself by playing to same old phrases over and over. I am not saying that you will forget. I am saying that you can move on and live in the moment, not in the past; living and reliving old past memories that only bring you down and cause you to feel many old emotions of guilt, anger, or hate. These feelings only keep you captive and hold you in a continuous pattern or loop of negative emotions.

I asked my husband Terry if I could share his story with you and he agreed that I could. He knows that his story may help someone else that might have similar feelings. He used to carry around the deepest feelings of guilt because of the dreams he had and the knowing he felt that he had killed people in another life, that he had beheaded them. He carried much guilt and depression over this. He thought he was just an awful person, that he was a bad person. Now he understands that he can let go of those feelings. He no longer has to have those negative feelings weighing him down. He understands and knows in his heart that it is all experience. He now understands that we are all on different paths. He has since moved on. It did not matter what I said or how I tried to help him, it was always up to him to let go of these feelings and free himself.

As you let go of these old emotions you allow yourself to expand and free yourself to experience life as it happens. So why keep yourself a prisoner? Each moment offers a new beginning. This is important that you know, repeat after me, each moment offers a new beginning. I like to sing this little song to myself, "Let it go, Let it go, Let it go." I sing it to the tune of "Let it Snow".

You may say it is not that easy. "You have not lived in my shoes." My response, no I have not lived in your shoes, nor you mine. It is as easy as you letting it go. Set your intent to do so. YOU are the one that controls you. You may be taking an antidepressant or other medications and if so, do not stop taking your medication without your Doctor's consent. That little pill may help you to feel better, but we are going to do some things that will really make the positive difference in your life. It begins with your desire to make a positive change in yourself, to embrace happiness and joy. It is time that we get started. Know that you can be happy! There are many, many people who desire to just be noticed, to be heard and to have happiness be a part of their lives. Please know, I am with you in spirit as you are reading these words and I want you to know that I have you in my heart and I feel your pain. I love you as you are in this very moment. You can be joyful! We are working on ourselves. None of us are perfect, that is something our society has dreamed up. What is perfect anyway? When you are sovereign unto yourself, you cannot be a victim any longer, a victim to yourself or to anyone else. Carrying and replaying our old negative junk around keeps us as the victim. We are held captive when we are unable to let go of our negative emotions and our ghosts of the past. We, each one of us holds the key to the lock of our cage door. If you want to unlock the cage door, it is YOUR choice. What are you waiting for? Take out your pretend key, unlock the cage door and let's continue on our path. Are you ready? You will begin to feel the expansion, the freedom, the instant you make the decision to FREE yourself. Ahhhhhh . . . doesn't that feel so much better? I must let you know that it does feel really good to empower ourselves in this manner, kind of like putting your PJ's own when you want to relax and not have any restrictions. The weights will begin to slip off immediately and you will feel so much lighter. It is your job to remind yourself that you are a sovereign individual. You do not have to make anyone else happy, that is their job. When we all do our job of empowering ourselves and being responsible, life can become so enjoyable! In this way you are not the victim nor are you trying to control another.

Affirmations

It is time to stop replaying any old self sabotaging words you may use on yourself. Quit. Stop. You are going to stop replaying any words that may have been used to criticize or belittle you and you are going to replace them with positive, uplifting words, words of encouragement, and words of acceptance. We are going to say positive affirmations to ourselves every day. We are going to believe those beautiful words. Affirmations can be any sentence that you say to yourself that reflect something positive about yourself. You may want to make a list of some positive things. For example, "I deserve to be happy." "I am going to have a positive outlook about today's events." "I am going to work and be happy." "This is my life and I am in control." "I am beautiful." It would be quite helpful to start keeping a journal of your thoughts and feelings each day as you begin to integrate changes in your life. You will be so surprised to see your progress and how you will change your thinking about yourself, others and life. Be sure to date each entry. If you feel like YOU want to make changes in your life, it needs to be your decision, not someone else's idea.

Let's recoup:

Unlock the cage door.
Be sovereign.
Let go of the past.
Know you are no longer a victim, take off the badge that says you are.
Make a list of positive affirmations, saying them aloud 1x daily, or
    as often as needed.
Write your feelings and emotions in your journal. Be sure to date
    your entries.

The Golden Nugget

When I talk about finding the golden nugget I am referring to getting past surface issues and finding the real lesson in everyday life experiences or those experiences that may seemed to have been difficult. These are situations that leave us angry, bewildered or sad and crying for example. Family, loved ones, close friends, co-workers and even strangers can give us learning opportunities. When these situations arise they usually give us a chance to learn and overcome. When we realize this lesson and find the "golden nugget", we get a free pass out of the situation occurring again. We will often find out things about ourselves that we need to be aware of. These could be things like, letting go of jealousy, being aware of letting the ego and pride get in our way, or it could be about learning to have compassion and understanding. You might be presented with a situation that could teach you about your inner strength or the power of forgiveness. It could be a lesson about loving yourself and others. Whatever the situation, consider it a learning opportunity for yourself, not a punishment. You may want to list any nuggets that you have discovered recently. Like any golden nugget, sometimes they are hard to find on the surface.

Controlling our thoughts

When we are able to control our thoughts we can make some really giant strides in our progress. Our brains are often referred to as "monkey brains" meaning they jump around from place to place. When we can control our brains and take the helm, the brain no longer keeps us like a ship on the ocean without any navigation. I am asking you to allow some new ideas into your psyche. You may be asking, what difference does it make what we think if we are not saying it out loud? I want you to realize that those thoughts of ours carry an energy vibration. We have either positive or negative thoughts. So in effect, we are raising or lowering our vibration. We are going a little deeper into what I call spirit science and I would ask that you continue to remain open minded. All is energy and as beings of energy, the emotions we allow into our being can either make us vibrate faster, lifting us up, or vibrate slower, bringing us down. The emotions of guilt, anger and hate are of a lower vibration whereas the emotions of love, compassion and understanding are of a higher vibration and thus make us feel lighter. The lighter we are the better we feel. It is important to be aware of the thoughts and emotions you allow into your mind. I had mentioned this earlier; we need to be responsible for our thoughts. We need to take responsibility for the thoughts that we choose to have. We will then begin to see where some of the thoughts that we have originated from. It is often just information that has been instilled into our brains at an early age, from our parents, family, the church, television, school and the list goes on. For many of us we have taken this information as truth and applied it without really thinking about it. It has been recycled in our brains over and over without any examination. It is time to be deliberate and look at the thoughts you allow in your brain. Thoughts carry emotion with them. I am not criticizing anyone's family, we all have ideas and ways of thinking that have been passed down from generation to generation. We are living in a time that is on the cutting edge of technology, but beyond that we are on the edge of knowing about ourselves in a more positive way. We are evolving our consciousness. We are remembering. We are continuing to learn about our world and its relationship to the rest of the universe.

If everything is energy then our thoughts are energy too. When we begin to monitor our thoughts and can make a choice to think another thought we start to gain control of our personal world. Our thoughts create our beliefs. Our beliefs cause us to have certain perspectives. It is through this lens that we "see" our reality.

All of the different religions would have you to believe in their view of creation and the one we often refer to as God. Organized religion is often times a way to control and manipulate through fear, shame and guilt. We have all been created by the one and that same creator created everything from the universe, the planets, the animals, the plants, the oceans and all the different peoples. We are all connected. We all have the same life force within our being. When looked at from this view point, we can see that ALL life is sacred. I am sacred. YOU are sacred. We are all sacred, cut from the same fabric of life. We are not separate from our Creator. We are all children of the ALL THAT IS.

Meditation

"In the attitude of silence the soul finds the path in a clearer light, and what is elusive and deceptive resolves itself in crystal clearness," as said by the great one, Mahatma Ghandi. We have been trained in our Western world to rely on the brain for our answers but it is the body that will react and give you the answer you seek. When you meet someone for the first time, do you not get an impression of that person at the gut level? Our brains are a most valuable analytical tool, but there is another part of ourselves that we are not recognizing and that is the fact that we are more than this body. We are the soul and the soul is eternal. It is important to know that you are more than this body, to recognize yourself as the soul. Our western culture has not placed value on the soul. On the other hand, much emphasis has been placed on the material world, of wealth, belongings and financial status. There is nothing wrong with money. It is a type of energy exchange, but somewhere things became out of balance and we failed to connect and listen to that still small voice within that is our 'divine self' speaking to us. It is not in words but in urgings, thoughts and knowing. When we take the time to train our brains to stop thinking, we can tap into that part of ourselves. You can call it whatever you like. When you begin to take the time and let go of the material world long enough to listen to that inner voice you are going to be quite surprised. Some call prayer talking to God and meditation listening to God. Maybe you have meditated before or maybe you tried and just gave up. Meditation allows you to go beyond the analytical mind and listen to your heart. The heart never lies. I encourage you to do this wonderful activity for yourself. All of the things that were on your mind will still be there when you return.

First you will need to turn off your cell phone. Post a note or let someone know you do not wish to be disturbed for a while. Find a comfortable place that you can be left alone. This can be in nature, the den or your bedroom; any place that you can relax and disconnect.

Get comfortable. You may wish to sit so that you don't fall asleep. You may want relaxing music or not.

I want you to relax, feel your body relaxing. Take a deep breath, let it out and relax a little more and begin breathing in through your nose and out through your mouth rhythmically. I like to breathe in white light. Imagine and see it with your mind, (the light of our Creator) breathe in through the nose, bringing it into my crown and down into my whole body and then breathing out any and all tensions of the day. Concentrate on your rhythmic breathing and just allow yourself to let go. Aim for 10 minutes, gradually going to 20 minutes and increasing as you want each day. This is a beautiful gift to yourself. It will lift your spirit in so many invaluable ways.

The Imagination

We have all used our imagination whether it was intentional or not, but for the most part we tend to leave the imagination with that time when we were children. That child is still a part of you and needs to be recognized. When you get an urge to sing, or dance, or tell a story, pick flowers, lie on the ground and gaze into the sky, do it. Do it with abandon. Just allow and enjoy those moments.

I have a friend who refuses to believe a "figment of his imagination" as he calls it. He is intentionally denying a beautiful and beneficial gift of our mind. It is through the imagination that many worlds have been traversed. Here is Einstein's quote about comparison of the brain and our imagination. "Analytical thinking can take you from A to Z but your imagination can take you anywhere." If you have ever observed children at play, they are adept at using the imagination. They become totally absorbed in their world of the imagination. We can all embrace our imaginations. It is through the imagination that we can access other dimensions of reality. A dimension is simply a frequency, not a destination. This is a BIG universe and anything is possible, anything. We just live here in this small neighborhood called Earth.

I want you to crack that mind open a wee bit more. This is your chance to see in your mind's eye, use your imagination, to create your world and your life as you would like it to be. Let it be so real in your mind that you have the emotions that go with it. Yes, I know that it may not be this way, the way you desire it to be at the present moment, pretend that it is so if even for a few moments and let it go, knowing that you are taking steps to allow this to happen. Dream the dream and send it out to the Universe. Allow it. Suspend your judgment and just allow.

Forgiveness

I must include forgiveness as one of the most sacred acts that I know. It is not only a gift to others it is one of the most wonderful gift to our selves. When we are able to forgive, our spiritual heart opens even more and the light of Creator comes flooding in.

Forgiveness deserves it very own page. It is through forgiveness that the spiritual heart opens and we are truly allowed to heal on all levels, as the spiritual heart is the portal allowing us to express true love and acceptance for ourselves and others. This is a gift that we can give to ourselves so easily if we just do it. It is often easier to forgive another than it is to forgive one's self. To forgive, as I had mentioned earlier is not to forget. When we forgive we open our hearts so that we may move forward and continue on a higher path. When we do not forgive we are holding a clamp down on our spiritual hearts. We are restricting ourselves. We are doing harm to ourselves when we cannot forgive. The spiritual heart, the heart chakra is the color green. Green is the color for healing. You will notice all of the green that is on Mother Earth, all of our vegetation, our trees, flowers and plants. It is at this point, at the fourth chakra, that our lower chakras, those of our physical survival, our sexual and creative abilities and our solar plexus joined with our higher spiritual chakras can come together and overlap with the higher dimensional colors. Forgiveness allows us to be the beings that we are at our core, beings of joy, love and light.

Loving Self

I would like to talk about loving yourself and explain it a little further. We have discussed controlling your thoughts and your words. We have discussed taking time for yourself and meditating, listening to your inner voice. We have discussed forgiveness, allowing your heart to open and be ready to receive. All of these are examples of the many ways of loving yourself. Taking care of the body, the vessel you use every day, the mind, through right thinking and the spirit through recognizing and knowing that you are more than this body, taking time in silence through meditation. I am talking about real love not the hooey, gooey emotional love that has feelings of attachment. I am not talking about loving yourself as from an ego perspective. Real love offers freedom and respect. Real love makes no demands. It just is. Real love leaves ego at the door. Sometimes we may hear people talking about someone being in "love with themselves," but, what they are probably meaning to say is that the person has an inflated ego. Real love is being caring and compassionate, responsible and respectful. Romantic love, well that is quite another story. Loving yourself may sound difficult, but it is not. Remember, how can we share what we do not have? Loving yourself is allowing yourself to be human. Loving yourself also means forgiving yourself for any perceived wrongs. Remember our creator is capable of everything imaginable and unimaginable, if certain experiences were not permitted they would not be allowed by creator. We are here to experience and learn, so stop judging yourself and others. We all have different learning scenarios. If we were meant to be perfect, why would we leave our true home and come to the world of physical manifestation? I want you to love yourself and know the happiness and joy that this world has to offer.

Gratitude

I cannot leave out nor forget the importance of gratitude in our everyday lives. When we live in a state of gratitude we are allowing ourselves to be open to receive. We have a chance to be grateful for even the smallest of details in our lives. It will only take a moment to say a simple blessing for the food we eat, the water we drink, the beautiful earth we live on. We can even thank the pain that may enter our bodies from time to time and ask to receive the message that it has brought to us. It may mean something as simple as we need to slow down and rest. It could mean we are not appreciating the present moment, but whatever it means, a simple recognition and appreciation is most helpful.

Synchronicities

All of us have had what seemed like a coincidence to happen to us in our lives. You are going about your daily activities and someone from the past pops into your thoughts, you go to the grocery store sometime within the next day or so and who do you "run" into; the person from your past that you had been thinking about. This has happened for a reason, not chance. Most of us refer to synchronicity as coincidence, but as I have mentioned earlier there are no coincidences. Webster defines a coincidence as a collection of two or more events or conditions, closely related by time, space, form or other associations which appear unlikely to bear a relationship as either cause to effect or effects of a shared cause, within the observer's or observers' understanding of what can produce what effects. That is the logical scientific definition. When looked at from the spiritual perspective it is clearly understood that the universe has conspired to assist us in "organizing" these two seemingly unrelated events on our behalf. There is a reason for such synchronicities to happen in our lives. I consider this to be one of the most wonderful of events! This is another opportunity that has been provided for us. The cause may not be apparent initially, but it is there if we take a moment to ponder and allow it to come forth. There is not one thing that is left to coincidence. Our world is not one way for some and not for others. It is up to us to take notice, pay attention, and allow the universe to assist us; to not only take notice but to ask for assistance.

These little synchronicities may happen without our even noticing if we aren't paying attention. You may see a billboard that has a message just for you. You may run into a long lost friend and you start a new business together. You may see two blue birds while you are driving. What messages are they saying to you?

You may need to remember how you felt seeing those certain words on the billboard, what meaning did they have for you? How did you feel seeing the two blue birds while driving? What was on your mind? Ask questions of yourself from a feeling standpoint and allow what you feel to come through. You will have to discern as to whether there is a message for you or not. Go with your gut.

The universe works in subtle ways so as not to "interrupt" our daily routines. As we are able to peel back the layers and get to our true being, we will remember that everything is connected.

Addiction

Although addiction may not be a tool that is recognized as something that is going to assist us on our path, it is something that I think all of us have seen in our lives whether it is ourselves or someone close to us who may have an addiction. It could even be our spouse or our children. Addiction, according to Louise Hay's book, "Heal Your Body", is the inability to love one's self. As we look around we can see there are many thoughts, imagined reasons why we should not love ourselves, which means there are many addictions to be had. It is not always drugs or alcohol. It could be exercise, diet, food, sex, shopping, cigarettes, reading; the list goes on and on. Although it is difficult for us to witness a loved one who is addicted to drugs or alcohol, it is not our life. We can offer our love and compassion, we can offer to assist, but we cannot make the choice for someone else to leave an addiction, it is up to the individual, always! How many times have we read about or have seen someone placed in detox or rehab only to escape and start back where they left off. I am not saying that we have to support, or be a co-dependent for the addict. Sometimes hitting rock bottom is where the light at the end of the tunnel is found. It does not mean you don't love someone if you say enough is enough. It does however mean that you care enough to care. What are you learning about yourself in your relationship with an addict? Remember you agreed to play the part of being in their lives while on the other side. Find the golden nugget. Seek it out.

Being sovereign is about taking responsibility for yourself. Remember do not depend on someone else for your joy and happiness. Blind faith, trust, knowing and believing that our creator knows what is best for our soul, all of these beliefs will be required. Dying may frighten us, but death is just another step onto the pathway of being. We are eternal beings of light! Shine on! Remember, you are a precious jewel. As you come to make peace and accept life and accept yourself, you will be able to embrace joy and happiness, knowing that everyone else is on their path. Once you accept yourself as the soul and know that your life has always been your choice, you can move forward, creating the reality you desire. When I say move forward I am referring to the fact that once you accept yourself as you are and accept others as they are and know that all is as it should be; you are FREE! JUST BE! God has given us quite the gift, yes? Enjoy it!

In Conclusion

I t is my sincere wish that we all have happiness and joy in our lives! I hope that you will be able to look at death from another perspective and remember that this is just a small part of the big picture. Peel back the hardened layers we as a society have placed upon ourselves and find the sweetness of you and the sweetness of this life, know that it is all good.

I have given you a glimpse into my journey through life as I have perceived it. I have shown you how my perceptions have changed. As my perception changed so did my world, my reality. We can all hang onto old beliefs, old ideas and old feelings, using them as our excuse, or we can make a choice to let them go. Live in this present moment, knowing that life is beautiful! Relax into this life and please know that our Creator has taken care of every little minute detail.

I hope that I will get to meet many of you who will read about my journey and you will become a part of my story and I yours. I look forward to our meeting with much anticipation.

Much love and many blessings, The Sherri One

I may be reached by email at serenityfarmretreat@gmail.com
Casey's Remembrance Video, YouTube Casey Tyler Fox.

You may make your reservation to come and stay or visit Serenity Farm Retreat via email or visit the web site at <u>www.serenityfarmretreat.com</u>

Bibliography

Hall, Judy, The Encyclopedia of Crystals (Fair Winds Press, Beverly, MA 2006)

Hay, Louise, Heal Your Body (Hay House Inc. Carlsbad, Ca 2009)

Miller, Robert M. D.V.M. Understanding The Ancient Secrets of The Horse's Mind (The Russell Meerdink Company, Ltd 1999)